# HAUNTED
# ST IVES

# HAUNTED
# ST IVES

IAN ADDICOAT

The
History
Press

First published in 2008 by Tempus Publishing

Reprinted in 2011 by
The History Press
The Mill, Brimscombe Port,
Stroud, Gloucestershire, GL5 2QG
www.thehistorypress.co.uk

British Library Cataloguing in Publication Data.
A catalogue record for this book is available from the British Library.

ISBN 978 0 7524 4542 7

Typesetting and origination by The History Press.
Printed in Great Britain

# CONTENTS

# ABOUT THE AUTHOR

Ian Addicoat is an established writer and researcher of the paranormal. He is honorary president of the Paranormal Research Organisation (PRO) (UK) and has investigated countless haunted properties, specialising in the South West. He has appeared on numerous television programmes, including *Most Haunted, Animal X* and *GMTV*, and is a partner in two companies specialising in ghost walks and paranormal events. Above all Ian prides himself on his rational approach to ghosts and the supernatural.

# ACKNOWLEDGEMENTS

A special thanks to The Paranormal Research Organisation for agreeing to me using certain information but mainly for keeping me sane and making me laugh lots. Also thanks to all my friends and fellow investigators in the organisation, for plenty of professional investigating but also fun and humour along the way.

A huge thanks also to everyone who contributed stories and information. I am eternally grateful to you all and only wish I could name and thank each and every one of you individually.

I would also like to thank all of my other friends and family, my parents, Debs, Alishia and Connor.

# INTRODUCTION

St Ives is described as 'a jewel situated at the south-western tip of Cornwall'. It is renowned for its golden beaches, charming harbour, crystal-blue waters, narrow cobbled streets, fisherman's cottages, surfing and many world-famous artists, not to mention the celebrated Tate Gallery.

However the town has also long been associated with a strong haunted heritage and reputation. Incredibly the local authorities still employed a professional ghost-layer right up until about 150 years ago, long after most other local towns had dispensed with the services of such dubious characters. The most famous of these uncertain individuals was the Revd William Polkinghorne, who came from St Ives and worked there in the early eighteenth century. He became most famous for allegedly laying the ghost of the infamous 'Wild Harris' from Kenegie Manor; a turbulent spirit who had long defied the powers of all the other clergy from the district. Harris was, at length, supposedly laid to rest by Parson Polkinghorne within the ancient ramparts on the Iron Age hill fort of Castle-an-Dinas.

There are dozens of so-called haunted properties in St Ives and the surrounding area. Perhaps much of this has to do with the fact that the town has a higher than average percentage of very old houses. One classic example of ghostly events took place in a house in central St Ives where residents reported that late at night they heard high-heeled footsteps raking across the bedroom floor, reverberating above. This was followed by a knocking at the door, though there was absolutely nobody in the property. Another of St Ives' more traditional legends is that of the 'Seven Whistlers'. It is said that if you hear these strange whistling noises at night it is a warning of coming tragedy to the listener or indeed the town itself. As with so many Cornish towns, St Ives is bursting with legends, folklore and haunted tradition and these are but the tip of the iceberg.

The town is also famous for the literary rhyme and riddle *As I was going to St Ives*:

> As I was going to St Ives
> I met a man with seven wives
> And every wife had seven sacks
> And every sack had seven cats
> And every cat had seven kits
> Kits, cats, sacks, wives
> How many were going to St Ives?

# HAUNTED ST IVES: AN A – Z

## Arts Club

Several people have told me that this building is haunted but unfortunately details are somewhat scarce. It is generally accepted, however, that a figure has been seen and voices have been heard on a regular basis. Many people visiting the building to attend one of its various events have reported strange sensations and a general feeling of dread.

## Atlantic Lane

About forty years ago an elderly gentleman used to live in a house situated near the top of this lane which leads up to the upper part of the town from the Downlong area. Unfortunately as the years went by he developed some problems with one of his legs and found it increasingly hard to walk, subsequently only being able to get around with the aid of a walking stick. Nevertheless, being a stout fellow with a reputation for stubbornness, he would walk resolutely down this lane nearly every single night on his way into the town centre. On punctually arriving at a local pub there, he would meet his friends for a drink and this was his way of socialising and getting out of the house. He would then spend an hour or so enjoying a drink before returning back to his home a while later. However, one night he failed to show up at the time he would normally have arrived and out of concern some of his friends went looking for him. Tragically they found him lying prone and dead in the lane. It transpired that he had stumbled and hit his head on a wall, to the side of the lane, and died from his injuries as a result of the impact, a dreadful accident.

Many people have reported over the years since, being in the lane and hearing loud, slow footsteps, yet nobody appears to be making them. They are unhurried and rhythmical sounds and after every second step people also hear the unmistakable tap of a stick. Quite a number of people have also suffered from sudden reported headaches whilst they are in the lane. Research reveals that they are always standing at the exact spot where the man fell to his death some forty years ago.

Above and left: *Arts Club*

*Atlantic Lane*

# Boots the Chemist

I was informed recently by a couple of ladies who worked here that this shop is allegedly haunted. Apparently many of the staff have commented on a strange atmosphere and peculiar sensations. The lift is also often said to start moving between floors, seemingly by itself. The ghost is claimed to be that of a fisherman, which is understandably a very familiar type of ghost in St Ives.

# Bullans Lane

It is said that years ago a young girl with learning difficulties lived in one of the houses here. She had serious behavioural problems and eventually was taken into care due to a very serious incident. The child had apparently pushed her mother down the stairs and seriously injured her. People living in the building since have described a presence on the stairs and a feeling as though someone is attempting to push them down the stairway. Fortunately nobody has ever actually fallen but some people have been so unnerved that they have moved out of the house soon after having such experiences. Some people have also described the voice of a young girl being heard in the area of the stairs and the upper floor.

*Boots the Chemist*

*Bullans Lane*

# Carbis Bay, Cliff

Here we have the unlikely tale of a cliff creature. It is described as a tall figure seen on the cliff path, which leads from the village to St Ives and from where one can observe stunning views across Carbis and St Ives Bays. When the character is seen, it moves in a dramatic swaying, jerking motion and transcends swiftly but unnaturally across the cliff path before vanishing over the edge. The body is described as being vaguely human-like in appearance but the head is like a pumpkin in shape, large and round.

It seriously does have to be one of the least likely stories I've heard, though the author Michael Williams, in his book *Supernatural in Cornwall*, describes some of the supposed chance meetings with the creature in the 1960s.

However, at least two more recent sightings have also come to light since the book was published. A person was in the area in recent years and described the figure as faceless and that it was jogging alongside him and his wife. They also described the figure as wearing long grey robes and although the creature was solid it appeared to cast no shadow despite it being a very sun-soaked afternoon. Also another witness described seeing the figure bending down and scratching at the floor before suddenly leaping up and jumping over the edge. When they nervously looked down to see where the thing had gone, there was nothing there!

# Carbis Bay, Endsleigh Guest House

The owners of this four-star-rated bed and breakfast told me that they have had spiritual activity here for some time. The structure was built in 1860 and according to them there seem to be at least three entities haunting the premises. These include two children and a woman – all apparently friendly and benign. The ghostly lady once woke one of the owners in the middle of the night by saying 'hello' in his ear! Many years ago the owner was a practising medium in Burslem in Stoke-on-Trent and so is well-versed in such paranormal activity. His partner has also heard the children playing upstairs and described sounds like people chatting. These usually are heard coming from a downstairs bedroom, which is built over the old garden area. Another regular phenomenon that occurs is that the doorbell is said to frequently ring at 4 a.m. The owners believe that this may be explained by servants who used to arrive here at that time, many years ago, this being at a time in history when the hotel was just a big house.

# Carbis Bay, Laity Lane

In one particular house here it is claimed that every time anything is done to the property such as renovation work or redecoration, ghostly shenanigans are reported. The building was said to have been a former counting house for the nearby mines before they closed.

Some of the most consistent phenomena include a feeling that is described as an 'unnatural coldness' that permeates the building even when the heaters are on full. Objects are described as mysteriously appearing and disappearing on regular occasions throughout the house. During one period of work a bowler hat was discovered under the floorboards in a room. This hat was placed on the nearby windowsill but kept vanishing, only to reappear elsewhere at a later time. It was believed that no living person could possibly have done this and one night the workers

*Castle Inn*

purposely left it in an agreed place. All witnessed this and left together. On returning the next morning the hat had moved. This had been in an empty house, a fact confirmed by all the witnesses present. As a result of this incident they decided to bury the hat in the garden but lo and behold the next morning it was back in the house again. Perhaps even stranger was the claim that on one occasion the hat fell into the fire and somehow managed to come out completely unmarked. Eventually the hat vanished altogether and this coincided with an end to the all too familiar coldness that had been reported therein.

There have also been sightings within the house, usually of a small, elderly man, wearing a bowler hat, in the same room where the hat was discovered. He is usually seen entering the room, glancing around and then quickly exiting. Occasionally he has been seen standing by a mantelpiece; although this particular mantelpiece was as ghostly as he was as no such structure was present in the house at that time.

# Castle Inn

This pub, often described by locals as 'definitely the best pub in town – especially if you're after real ale', is reputedly haunted by Maud, a prostitute who allegedly resided in the building at the beginning of the twentieth century. In particular she is active in the back rooms of the pub where her rented room was apparently situated, and also in the cellar areas. She has been up to all kinds of mischievous pranks over the years and several independent landlords have confirmed their belief that the pub is haunted. Some of the antics associated with her misbehaviour have included doors mysteriously opening by themselves, objects being moved and turning up in peculiar places and things going wrong with barrels of beer. In particular, clips left on real-ale barrels often go missing and usually turn up in the bin which is at completely the opposite end of the bar. They have also been known to turn up in other unlikely places.

Many of the locals are fully aware of Maud's reported ghostly presence, especially in the loos, where she is often claimed to play with hand dryers and other electrical products.

# Chysauster Ancient Village

This amazingly preserved Iron Age settlement was originally occupied as early as the second century AD by local Cornish tribes. Their settlements would have been largely self-sufficient and the village consisted of eight stone-walled homesteads known as 'courtyard houses'. This style of prehistoric dwellings, like houses lining a village street, was peculiar to the Land's End peninsular and the Isles of Scilly. They would have grown crops and cereals and kept animals such as sheep, goats and hens. The area would have consisted of a number of stone-built houses, with a stone-paved open central courtyard, surrounded by a number of thatched rooms; the whole complex enclosed by a stone wall. There are also the remains at the site of a typical 'fogou' underground passage, so familiar in the area.

In 2005 a team of psychic investigators paid a visit and came up with the following information, mainly through dowsing. It should, though, be pointed out that this is in many ways unsubstantited information:

*House One*
The psychic, that I will for convenience call 'M', picked up the presence of two females: a mother and daughter, aged about thirteen or fourteen. They were apparently happy and they had lived in this 'House'. M sensed that the mother may have attended to the sick.

Behind the main room was a small area that they felt had been used as a storeroom for their grain. M also sensed a long tunnel, leading to a larger room; she could also see lots of pitchers and bowls containing pilchards, grain and possibly dried meats, saying that this area would have been guarded and the entrance covered by a large stone.

Moving to another small area, one investigator had a sharp pain in the back of his neck and another reported a headache, reporting that she did not like the feel of the area.

One team member was dowsing and found ley lines and energy lines, crossing the area where the people had developed a headache and experienced a pain across the neck.

M then revealed that she had picked up on the presence of 'Hetty', the spirit of a young girl, who is a resident ghost in this home, commenting how it was 'nice to have had her amongst us'.

*House Two*
Dowsing results here revealed that this area would have been used as an animal shed, housing goats, wild boar, sheep, hens and cows. Adjacent to this was a feeding area for the animals. One person reported a pain in her side and this went when she left the area.

M felt that Hetty was telling her to go elsewhere, unfortunately being unable to establish why.

*Chysauster ancient village*

## House Three

In this round house there were several small rooms leading off from the main courtyard. Once again the team carried out dowsing and revealed the presence of a male and a female who they felt were very interested in their activities. In one small room M could see a woman giving birth, she went on to describe also seeing small bowls and a curved knife.

In another room a male investigator picked up on an adult male and a young boy and he felt that the older male was showing the younger boy how to do something. He also had the feeling that something was 'strung up' and further felt that the boy was being shown how to skin an animal and cut up the carcass for food.

Overall, then, they picked up on some interesting information but Chysauster is a setting that is not necessarily known for paranormal activity. Indeed the results achieved during the investigation did seem to suggest that this was more about information than anything especially supernatural.

# Clotworthy's

In High Street, on the corner opposite Belmont Terrace, is a clothes shop which used to be called Clotworthy's. The name is still etched into the entrance porch. This was a well-known

*Chysauster ancient village*

men's outfitter with a sinister reputation and a building that has supposedly been haunted for many years. Back in the 1980s there was a very strange incident involving a young shop worker. He was alone in the premises one late morning when he suddenly felt an unbearable coldness encompassing him. At the same time he happened to glance up and observed a man who was entering into the shop. He felt an almost instantaneous icy cold feeling envelope the room and he could also detect that the strange man was staring at him in a manner that could only really be described as malevolent. This peculiar gentleman then began to cross the shop, heading in his general direction but then veered off and suddenly headed off up the stairs and in the direction of a changing room. The young man failed to describe him when asked later, saying it was almost as if he was faceless. The young man was so unnerved by this peculiar visitor that he fled the shop to get help from passers by, as he certainly didn't wish to be left alone with this sinister fellow. When he returned with others in accompaniment, he was stunned to find that the shop was deserted. This was evidently impossible because he had not moved any further than the doorway and there was only one exit.

A report of this peculiar event was transcribed in the local newspaper at the time and gained a great deal of local public interest. However, it does appear that activity has not been limited to just this one event. A young lady informed me, during her attendance on a ghost walk, that a friend of hers had recently resided in a flat above the shop and had often heard footsteps in the middle of the night. Supposedly this has happened to others as well.

*Clotworthy's*

# Cornerways Guest House

This solid granite building, situated in Downlong – the oldest part of St Ives – was built in 1837 in the middle of a labyrinth of cobbled lanes used as fisherman's cottages. It has been a guesthouse for over fifty years and has recently been renovated. This building is also well known for being where the author Daphne du Maurier, famous for the book *Jamaica Inn*, stayed, though I am sure that nobody is claiming that she herself haunts the property.

I was reliably informed that some people who have stayed here have awoken to hear banging and crashing. Some other former residents also stayed here and had their own abnormal experiences. On one occasion they left the house and returned much later to discover that glasses had been smashed onto the floor, yet nobody had been in the building. Another lady stayed in the bedroom and became very nervous and anxious and was later told that it was in fact haunted.

Above and below: *Cornerways Guest House*

# Cottages

People attending my St Ives Ghost Walks have told me independently about two separate holiday cottages in St Ives where some very strange occurrences have happened.

## Cottage One

On the first day of their stay at one particular cottage, a family experienced seeing several strange lights, observed with the naked eye. Shortly afterwards the husband went out on his own. Later that afternoon his wife heard the patio door making a sound as if someone was coming in and assumed it was her husband arriving back. However when nobody appeared and she later learnt that he had not been back at all, she felt very unnerved. That night the rest of the family went to bed and heard peculiar voices from downstairs. It was as if a party was taking place or that people were talking and yet there was evidently nobody there. A light was clearly on and yet they were sure it had been turned off. At this point they went downstairs to investigate and both heard a voice as if someone was standing by the light switch. Naturally enough they were quite unnerved and were uncomfortable staying there from then on.

## Cottage Two

People staying at another cottage saw a strange black shape moving around on regular occasions. The form was like that of a figure and sightings were often followed by peculiar dancing lights. Nobody was ever in the area at the time of events and so they were convinced that this was paranormal activity.

# Cripplesease Mine

This is one of my favourite places, situated in the parish of Towednack, and I must confess to a strange affinity for old Cornish mine buildings perhaps because several of my ancestors on my father's side were indeed Cornish miners. The construction here is a particularly fine example of an engine house but unfortunately there is no consistent information about whether the mine was Reeth Consols or Wheel Reeth but it is believed to have been used to extract cassiterite (black tin), employing as many as 155 people until 1867.

The moorland area directly around the engine house is a place where people often walk their dogs and come to photograph the buildings. Many people report an eerie feeling and strong impressions of being watched. There have also been quite a lot of people who have reported peculiar sounds, almost as if there are people still working the mine. This has included voices, hustle and bustle, the clanking of tools and horse's hoof beats.

# Digey

Many years ago, there was apparently a fire in a building here. I have been told that two young children died in the fire and they are now said to haunt the upstairs part of the building. Also nearby is a house where several independent residents have claimed to see a ghostly old man. He is usually observed standing at the foot of a bed. Others have just described the house as a 'very eerie' place.

Right and below: *Cripplesease Mine*

*Digey*

*Downalong, oldest house*

# Downalong, Oldest House

It is believed that this cottage, near the Wharfside, was built in 1443 and in 1993 Prince Charles paid it a visit whilst in the town. A few years ago, when this building came up for sale, two young men arranged to stay in the empty house. Apparently they were so scared by events that they ran out of the dwelling. They are reluctant to give details but stress it was a genuine experience.

I also had some people e-mail me after attending a St Ives Ghost Walk and they said 'We were staying in the oldest house in St Ives and did experience footsteps, moving chairs and weird dog-like smells.'

Left and opposite:
*Fore Street*

# Fore Street

There used to be a pub here on the corner with St Andrews Street, called the Tap House (also later called the Globe and possibly the Red Lion). It must have been a fair-sized establishment as it was described as having 'three good parlours, twelve lodging-rooms hung with bells and two beer and wine cellars' and in 1798 was also described in the following words: 'This inn, the situation and accomodation of which are very superior to any other in the town, is commonly used by the gentlemen travelers and others resorting to it and is well calculated to command the whole of that and and extensive business.' It was owned by the Edwards family and had previously been their family home and sadly burned down in 1898 after having been a dwelling house for a few years. One of the Edwards family, Hugh (not the news reader!) is said to have haunted the pub. One day he was out riding his horse in the nearby countryside when they both fell down a mineshaft and died. He was buried in the family vault at the nearby church

wearing, naturally enough, a suit of clothes. Years later, the next time the vault was opened his clothes had disappeared except for his riding boots which looked as good as new. It was claimed that his spook haunted the Old Tap House pub and heavy footfalls, like someone wearing boots, were often heard at night. Three sharp and loud raps on a bedroom door would then follow. It was said to sound just like a riding whip and of course was caused, it is claimed, by the ghost of Hugh Edwards.

Another shop in St Ives (15 Fore Street) is also apparently haunted. This premises, which for many years used to be R. T. Hollows & Sons, now belongs to the same company that now owns Knill House. It is an innocent enough place in terms of appearance, though nevertheless some of the staff feel that it is haunted. A correspondent, who had admittedly only worked there a couple of times, told me that the haunted reputation was well known amongst staff and that many of them were very unnerved by the various strange events that had occurred there.

# Guildhall/Dead Man's Walk

Adjacent to Boots the chemist and leading past the Guildhall is a small, dark and dare I say creepy back lane. This path, it is said, was once the route that condemned prisoners were taken on their way to be hung. The unfortunate victims were then taken to an area near the Town Square and behind what is today 'Lanhams'. There they would be swiftly despatched at the gallows in front of a baying crowd. In 1549 during the Prayer Book Revolution the Provost Marshall, Sir Anthony Kingston, came to St Ives and invited the Mayor, Mr John Payne, to lunch at the old George and Dragon, which stood at the west side of the marketplace facing the church. He asked the mayor to have the gallows erected during lunch. After lunch the mayor and the provost marshall walked down to the gallows, the provost marshall ordered the mayor to get up on the gallows where upon the mayor was hanged for being a Roman Catholic – a charming episode commemorated on a plaque on the wall of the Catholic church four centuries later.

Often nicknamed 'Dead Man's Walk' the lane is said to be very atmospheric and people are often claiming to have strange feelings here. The simplest is a feeling of being followed, as if an unseen person is following them down the lane. There are other people who have claimed to hear footsteps and when they have nervously turned around there is nobody there. However a few have claimed to see a dark shadowy figure moving down the lane behind them. A lot of people describe negative emotions, including fear, anxiety, expectation, depression and desolation, claimed to possibly be consistent with the feelings the condemned men would have suffered on their way to the gallows. There are even those who have claimed to feel tautness around the throat, akin to a rope being tightened. Perhaps much of this could be put down to autosuggestion, expectancy, or to the simple fact this is a dark, creepy back lane. However, on 2 October 2007 a very strange episode occurred to various people on a ghost walk here. I have led a lot of people along this way previously and, apart from a few isolated incidents, nothing terribly dramatic has happened. However, on this one particular night all that changed. There was a lady, that from her accent I took to be from North American origin, who had a very pronounced encounter that night. All of a sudden she appeared to be affected by something dramatically and eventually was so disturbed she began to pass out. Some of the group, including myself, managed to catch her and I carried her to a nearby wall to take a seat. She was visibly paled and shocked and had been obviously distressed deeply. Her symptoms wee akin to how psychics describe so-called psychic attacks. This poor lady was completely unwilling to go back through the same area and so I had to support her and lead her around. As soon as we got away from the lane she was fine and there were no further incidents relating to her. At the end of the tour I spoke with her again and she seemed level-headed and not an obvious candidate for hype or attention seeking. Then several of the other independent attendees came and spoke to me and reported their own feelings from their time in that lane. These included feelings of being pushed and cajoled, a lady at the back hearing a rustling like clothing, tightness on the throat, headaches, pinching and prodding and very hot sensations. For so many it was difficult to dismiss and to me could be either explained as either mass hysteria or something very peculiar.

Incidentally, there is a funny legend related to the hangings in St Ives. Some claim that when public executions were still taking place, the way the authorities would announce to the town that it was about to occur was for someone to climb the church tower and to add an extra chime to the town clock at the appointed hour. That way everyone knew what was about to take place and those ghouls who wanted to watch the gory spectacle could come and do so. Today it is claimed that if you are walking around St Ives and hear the church clock chime on the hour, but hear one extra, it is said to be the sign of a guilty conscience!

*Dead Man's Walk*

*Guildhall*

# Halsetown Inn

This is a typical Cornish pub and a bit of a locals' secret, situated on the scenic back road between Nancledra and St Ives. With its interesting Regency façade, the Halsetown Inn is described as 'a proper local ... serving real beer and real food and well worth a stop off visit'. The pub dates from 1832 and has recently been refurbished with period pictures and is a very charming location, with open fires and a fantastic Cornish range. Miners would have frequented the pub in years gone by and the local MP and mine-owner James Halse in fact built the pub and village. Eighty granite cottages and the inn were laid out and built by Halse to accommodate his growing workforce of miners. Each house had its own very small plot of land and this was considered enough to encourage the residents to vote for him, as he wished to be the only MP returned for the Borough of St Ives, which then consisted of St Ives, Towednack and Lelant. The village was completed in good time for polling day – 11 December 1832.

*Halsetown Inn*

As for the inn itself, there are rumours that it is haunted and a few years ago I received a letter from a gentleman from Australia. He wrote to say 'I was told some years ago, by a reputable source, that he had seen very clearly an apparition of a woman, in nineteenth-century dress, on the first floor of the Halsetown Inn, just outside of St Ives'. Funnily enough since then I have been told a similar story from another source entirely. This was a local man who was convinced the pub is haunted and referred to a Victorian woman.

## Hayle, Chip Shop

A building that used to be Hubbard's Fish and Chip Shop was previously used as a place to sell pottery and ornaments. Next door there was an old-fashioned, beamed house. Banging would be heard coming from upstairs in that particular building and this was followed by heavy footsteps. These were all heard on a frequent basis in the house. The floorboards would often be heard creaking heavily and then footsteps would be heard as if someone was ascending the stairs – stairs that incidentally are no longer there! A local medium visited and supposedly sent the presence away. However, years later the ghost returned and the same footsteps were heard once more. Also things have been found to move around and latches pulled on doors by unseen hands.

## Hayle, Harbour Area

There is a particular council house, near the harbour area of Hayle, that is claimed to be haunted even though it is less than forty years old. Previous witnesses have described an elderly man who is seen

*Hayle, harbour area*

sitting next to the fireplace. His clothes are described as appearing to be from the era of the 1960s and several different people have seen him on a number of separate occasions. He is believed to be a somewhat friendly spook and just seems grounded to this home, possibly wondering why strangers are in his house. He is believed to be a gentleman called Harry who lived here when the house was first built in the mid-sixties. He had lived there for several years and everyone who had known him referred to him as a perfect gentleman; pleasant, friendly, warm-hearted and generous. He sadly died in the house in 1969 after suffering from a heart attack. After several days his neighbours noticed they hadn't seen him and thus called in the police. When two officers arrived at the house they were forced to break in and sadly found Harry slumped in his chair, next to the fireplace.

## Hayle, Harbour

In a particular house in the harbour area of Hayle there is a peculiar yet regular phenomenon. At almost exactly 9.00 p.m. every night, the unpleasant smell of fish is usually detected by whoever is present in the house at the time. The owners were sure this was no natural smell and after a great deal of investigation ruled out all possible factors. However, coincidentally a previous resident had been a fisherman and 9.00 p.m. was the time he would usually come home when he returned from fishing trips to sea. Neighbours, who had known him very well when he had still been alive, confirmed this fact.

# Hayle House

In a rural farmland area, just outside of Hayle and close to the A30 bypass lies another building with a peculiar story and series of extraordinary sightings, both ghostly and possibly UFO in origin, thus suggesting perhaps an area of paranormal significance. On the land there is a farmhouse dating to about 1800 and it lies in the path of what is claimed to be a ley or energy line. These points of alignment are said by new age theorists to be places that give off special energies or magnetic or electrical forces, often associated with ghosts, the paranormal and UFOs. Furthermore the house also stands on mining land, with several mine buildings and disused shafts in the surrounding countryside and it is suggested that before the house was built, there lay a former counting house on the same site. Indeed Hayle was home to two of the three largest mine-engine foundries in the world.

The most consistent sighting at the premises is that of a lady in black, seen gliding across a nearby lane. Multiple witnesses, throughout a long period of time, have seen the figure and the independent descriptions do appear to show strong corroborative evidence. The lady wears what appears to be an old-fashioned, long flowing black dress, complete with dark shawl and white hat. The appearance of the clothes suggests that she could be dated to the late seventeenth century, though the black colouring is certainly of particular interest.

Above the house there have also been numerous UFO sightings since the 1980s, up to the present day.

# Hayle Shop

A family-run shop here in Hayle experienced an angry outburst of apparent poltergeist activity during a period in the 1980s. A particular local family moved into the premises and almost immediately suffered an array of strange phenomena. In the first instance they kept detecting a multitude of peculiar odours. The olfactory phenomena included strong old-fashioned tobacco, a smell like sandalwood (a fragrance that ironically many psychics claim can assist in removing spirits from a house) and especially a very unpleasant smell described as being like that of mouldy bread. They also described continual and pronounced drops in temperature in a specific part of the shop and yet could not explain this as the heating would be on and the rest of the shop was warm. Then things progressed and they began to hear an assortment of noises throughout the building. The first sound they heard was a 'mooing' as if a cow was in the shop. Of course this was not the case, however the premises had previously contained a dairy in the lower section, indeed where the sounds were emanating from, something they did not find out until long after the described events had begun taking place. They also heard noises as if someone was working, indeed sawing or sanding, and again they later discovered that there had been a workshop in the relevant area. The other noise they heard on a frequent basis was the sound of a young female, this being when there was nobody around. However things became

*White Hart Hotel, Hayle*

more disturbing still when objects around the house kept being strewn around. This included ornaments, documents, crockery, but most incredibly, items that had been locked and deposited in a safe and also the contents of a fish tank were emptied. Peculiar dancing lights were also seen floating across the room by the family.

After a while the goings on had become so disturbing that the family felt they had little choice but to call in a local priest who duly carried out an exorcism. However the ritual proved unsuccessful as activity continued and so they also called in a local medium, who claimed the haunting was being carried out by a young girl who was troubled as she did not understand that she had died and did not like the family being in the house. Eventually the psychic appeared to have more success as the activity abated and the haunting appeared to disappear.

## Hayle, White Hart Hotel

The White Hart Hotel stands proudly in the centre of this historic town, in Foundry Square, and is a prominent Grade II Listed building. The Harvey family, of great fame in the town, owned the building and ran it as a hotel as early as 1838. Henry, the famed shipyard and foundry owner, built it for his sister Jane. Richard Trevithick, famous local inventor of the high-pressure steam engine, was married to a former manager of the hotel.

Today, the White Hart remains a central part of Hayle's history and a perfect base for touring historic West Cornwall. The hotel has been extensively refurbished and careful renovations have kept the classical edifice intact, maintaining the elegance and charm of its Victorian origins. The White Hart's Gallery Restaurant is lavishly decorated with a number of fine paintings and the hotel's large collection of portraits help maintain the ambience of this historic hotel. Today it serves as a twenty-five-room hotel with a bar and restaurant, aptly called Harvey's. Ghost stories abound – especially in Room 9 – however the details are notoriously tricky to pin down.

# Hospital

A local man, who was well known for his spiritualist beliefs, told me the following story. In 1976 this gentleman was admitted to a local hospital for a relatively straightforward operation

*Hospital*

to remove an ulcer. Unfortunately complications set in during the operation and he developed what is known as 'Farmer's lungs'. In the end he became very seriously ill and was described as being effectively dead for three days and ended up being in hospital for several months as a result. He described how at the time he seemed to get a sense for things that were going to happen; for example he would often detect an odour or 'a smell of death' which was usually as a prelude to another patient passing away. Ultimately he ended up having another operation to rectify his problems and when he woke up after the procedure, it was to an empty ward and empty beds, except for one lady who he could see sitting in a nearby chair. He described her as being beautiful, tall and wearing a green and white striped dress uniform. She spoke to him and said 'the trouble you gave us' but it was almost as if she didn't move her mouth. Soon afterwards a nurse came over asking how he was and pulled a screen around him but appeared to be oblivious to the other female.

The next morning he discovered that there had been no such lady visiting him, however. The story in the hospital was that twice previously, other patients had seen the same lady. Both of them had similarly been very unwell and had not been expected to live. However, the lady visited them when they did survive and the staff have called her Sister Patricia. It appears that she is a benign and friendly soul, believed to have been a former member of staff here at a time when they wore such nursing uniforms. Although the building was also previously used as a convent and some have suggested this may in fact be the ghost of a former nun.

# The Island

The following story is possibly St Ives' most famous tale and has appeared in countless books over the years. Admittedly there have been a number of slightly different interpretations of the main story within different publications. Many years ago a ship got into terrible difficulties as it was entering St Ives Bay and ended up floundering off the island. Eventually it was wrecked off the rocks at the back of the island and many people tragically lost their lives as the waves surged over the ship and it began to sink. A group of brave local fishermen, seeing the danger, headed out in their fishing boats in a courageous attempt to save the people in obvious peril. However as a young woman was being passed between the stricken vessel and the rescue boat, she was carrying a baby. Desperately the child slipped from her grasp, plummeting to the frothing sea below and she lost her infant son in the raging water, the child doomed to a watery fate. Subsequently the devastated mother was brought into the other boat alone and as the vessel arrived at shore, she immediately leapt from the boat and began wretchedly searching the coastline for her child's body and she continued this forlorn search for several days and nights. Often her sad figure was witnessed walking the island alone late at night, clutching a lantern in her hands, her eyes trained onto the rocks. The child had of course tragically drowned and it is said that soon after, once she accepted the child's fate, his mother also passed away. This, it is claimed, was as a result of the shock, grief and the trauma involved in losing a beloved child and from the sheer exertion involved in endlessly searching in the cold and elements for several days.

It is claimed that the mother's ghost has been searching ever since for her lost child. Late at night the figure of a lady, wearing an old-fashioned, long flowing white dress is often seen walking the cliff paths or traversing down the rugged rocks of the island, carrying an old-style lantern, gripped into her fist. She is known locally as 'The Lady of the Lantern' and her ghost is said to be endlessly and hopelessly searching. She vanishes when approached and is seen especially on stormy nights and her appearance is said by many to be a portentous signal of

*Island Road*

coming ocean disaster. There have been countless rumoured sightings over the years of either the figure, or sometimes just a light, which appears to be very similar to the type of glow given off by a lantern, as if it was slowly moving across the rocks. I would imagine that a lot of the lights could be explained as natural phenomena, such as torches, cigarettes, reflections, moonlight, etc. However, I well remember a ghost walk a few years ago when myself and twenty witnesses all saw, from our position overlooking Porthgwidden Beach, a flickering light slowly moving across the rocks. We headed over to the location and the whole time we could still clearly see the light still shining. Incredibly as we approached we saw it vanish in front of our eyes and could not really come up with an obvious explanation. This was observed on the eastern side of the island, where indeed traditionally the lights are claimed to have been seen.

Some stories claim that on the night after the poor lady was buried, this being in the nearby graveyard (claimed to be Barnoon Cemetery), her ghost was seen drifting over the graveyard wall, across the beach and then onto the island itself. Clearly her spirit was not at rest and she was then seen searching for her child for several hours, before returning to the graveyard. This she has been allegedly doing ever since. However, my own belief is that this part of the story is at best artistic licence, as nobody that I am aware of has ever claimed to see such a sight.

Indeed this does seem to be a consistent theme with this particular story, as all too often seemingly made-up tales have appeared to assumedly add entertainment to the more familiar parts of the famous story. For example there are several publications that claim that if people go up to St Nicholas' Chapel, on the summit of the Island, at the stroke of midnight and walk around it twelve times, the Lady of the Lantern's ghost will immediately appear to them. Similarly another such story claims that by visiting the same chapel at midnight and shouting out 'White Lady' three times you might expect to drop dead. Obviously there is unlikely to be any reality to such outlandish superstition – especially as this is something that the local youth population have tried on a regular basis and no casualties have occurred to my knowledge and I have certainly never seen, on any occasion, an ambulance driving up the hill of the island at just after midnight!

Also on the island is another seemingly tall tale, indeed perhaps the least likely haunting in St Ives. The claim is that a headless horseman roams the so-called Island late at night, said to be a man on a large horse and typically carrying his head under his arm. The story has been around for many years; but perhaps not surprisingly I have never met anyone who claims to have actually seen this. Chances are that this has either been completely made up or is a misinterpretation akin to 'Chinese whispers' about the story of the Phantom White Horse of Island Road, described in the next section.

A story which is more likely to be genuine is that of ghostly monks. A small group of between three and five cowled and hooded figures have been seen walking up the hill of the Island towards St Nicholas' Chapel. This has usually been known to occur during daylight hours. When the ecclesiastical brethren get to the building they are seen to go straight through the closed wooden door and to vanish. It is possible that monks may have visited this area prior to the dissolution of the monasteries in the sixteenth century.

# Island Road/Porthgwidden Beach

For over six years I have led groups of people on the ghost walks of St Ives and a mainstay of the tour has been a well-known local story about a phantom white horse, centring on an area of Porthgwidden Beach and Island Road. I have known this story for many years and it is my favourite local ghost story.

However, when I started telling this story during ghost walks I genuinely never expected to find people regularly reporting to have actually heard the sounds of horses hoof beats. Yet I would estimate that on average every three to four tours that I lead somebody claims to hear exactly this. I would like to point out that this is not seemingly related to widespread autosuggestion, as I do not pass on any details in advance. The way this story works is that I stop the groups at the beginning of Island Road and explain that a noise is apparently heard in the street. I then ask them politely to listen as carefully as they can for any peculiar noise they might hear as they walk along. I also ask them to keep anything to themselves until prompted to do otherwise and to stay as quiet as possible in order that they won't miss anything important. We then walk down the street and stop above Porthgwidden Beach. At this point I ask people to tell me about anything they might have heard and then, and only then, do I proceed to tell the story, which is more or less on the following lines:

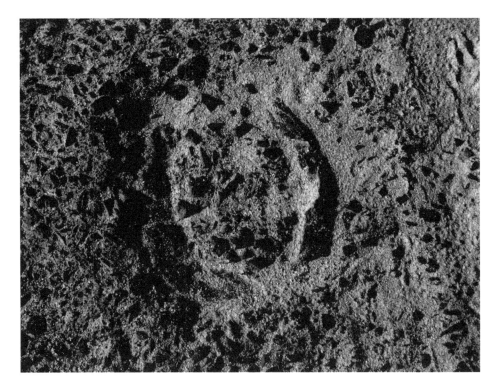

Above and below: *Porthgwidden Beach*

About 200 years ago in St Ives there lived a man who went by the name of Birch. He owned what everyone described as a beautiful white horse and he was so proud of the equine beast that the horse accompanied him almost everywhere he went. Indeed most nights, as dusk fell, the pair would be regularly seen riding down Island Road and then they would venture further down onto nearby Porthgwidden Beach. Once there, Birch would dismount from his horse and go for a quick swim in the bay, leaving his beloved companion poised alone on the beach awaiting his return. They would carry out this same ritual almost every single night and naturally they became a very familiar sight to locals. However, one fateful night, a long time after they would have usually left the shoreline, people walking past the sands saw the horse still standing there alone, with no apparent sign of Birch. It later transpired that the cruel waves of St Ives Bay, which had been the location for so many victims over the centuries, had claimed yet another new soul. The ocean currents had got too much for Birch and so he had succumbed to the current even though he was notoriously a strong swimmer. He had seemingly gotten into terrible difficulties and had wretchedly drowned. It is said that the horse was so determined to remain waiting for him that he stubbornly stood forlornly on Porthgwidden, in anticipation of his owner's return. In the end people had to physically drag and manhandle him from the beach and he was apparently taken to a stables nearby where he was well looked after and generously taken on by the stable's owners. Indeed the horse lived for several more years, before subsequently dying of old age.

Thus the sad story might have come to an end, however almost to the very day that the white horse died, the town of St Ives had a new ghost story. Many people claimed that they had been in the area of Island Road, as it was just beginning to get dark, when they saw a white horse slowly trotting down the street in the direction of Porthgwidden Beach. Yet on further investigation the steed appeared to have vanished. Incredibly in the early days hardly a week went by without such a sighting taking place and there were a whole host of people who apparently saw this familiar apparition. Stranger still was the fact that often, on nights when the horse had been seen in such a way, a little later on people saw what was apparently the same horse heading in the opposite direction. These other witnesses would indeed see this, heading back down Island Road. There was a marked difference though, as on the return journey there appeared to be a figure sat on the horse's back. Furthermore a number of the witnesses who alleged to have seen this, claimed that they had known Birch, the owner of the horse, and stated unquestioningly that the figure they saw, mounted on the steed, was none other than Birch himself. So St Ives new ghost story was that the horse was retuning to Porthgwidden Beach, collecting his owner and the two of them, then as ghosts, were heading back the way they always had and the way they surely would have done if this tragedy hadn't taken place. Such sightings continued for many years and were said to have been incredibly frequent. However, in the main they do seem to have diminished in recent years and very few people have claimed to see such a thing of late.

In modern times the experiences seem to have evolved into more commonly an audio phenomenon. Numerous people have been walking along the street here when they have suddenly stopped in their tracks and turned in astonishment because they were absolutely sure that they had heard the unmistakeable sounds of horse's hoof beats coming up behind them in the direction of the Island! Naturally they swing around; but there is nothing present and they are left feeling bemused. This has become a very well-known occurrence and it seems that hardly a week goes by without there being someone who claims to have heard this.

I wish to repeat that on average every three to four ghost walks that I take, somebody will mention this very noise as something they themselves have heard, this being when I ask if anyone heard anything whilst they were in the street. While I realise that many people may have misinterpreted other sounds or even had prior knowledge of the story and be victim to autosuggestion, all I can say is that even if only a tiny percentage of them have actually heard horse's hoof beats, it is still rather a lot of people. I have also known a lesser amount of people claim to have felt something speeding past them; or the sound of a horse sighing, a swishing tail or whinnying, also in Island Road.

## Knill's House, Fore Street

A while ago I received an e-mail from a young lady who at the time was working in a surf shop in St Ives. She said that the shop is allegedly haunted and was wondering if I knew anything about it as she was intrigued to find out any information.

The surf shop was called Prosurf and though it did not have a sign outside, it was identified by a large yellow 'Kangaroo Poo' flag in the window and used to be called G-Spot. The full address is Knill House, 50 Fore Street, St Ives. It is towards the Sloop Inn end of Fore Street, furthest from the harbour and appears to face east. The building used to be John Knill's house, though unfortunately the board that used to be on the front of the shop now apparently just lays upstairs collecting dust. Passers by who might appreciate the historical value of this property can no longer see it. A colleague of the person who wrote to me, and who used to live above the shop, claims to have seen a ghost at the shop and the lady herself said that sometimes when she was alone late at night she would hear footsteps when she knew nobody was there. This is all very intriguing because there was a famous ghost story about this very premises relating to the nineteenth century. It claimed that a 'well-dressed' lady haunted the place. One particular lady who allegedly often visited that house as a child is documented as stating that she remembered the fear of the inhabitants as they passed the door of this room after dark.

## Knill Monument

In 1782 John Knill, a famed local customs officer, paid for and erected a very visible mausoleum, also known as Knill Steeple on Worvas Hill, just outside St Ives. The structure is a triangular pyramid of hewn granite, 50ft high and containing within its base a cavity large enough for a single interment. Towering skywards in courses of cut blocks of local granite, the unique looking pyramid is capped with metal and has a lightening conductor. Also a low guard wall of granite was constructed in 1829 to protect the foundations. There is also an arch in the base giving access to the cavity but this has always been sealed up except during the memorial ceremony, described below. On one face is carved the word 'Resurgam', with the coat of arms and Motto (*Nil Desperandum*) of John Knill. The second face bears the inscription 'I know that my Redeemer liveth' while the third side is inscribed 'Johannes Knill 1782'.

Knill had intended to be buried there, as he 'abhorred the practice of burial within the body of the Church' despite the fact that this practice was the norm at the time. In addition, the churchyard was already overcrowded and he saw this as a healthier alternative. However, his plans never came to fruition, because the strategy had to be abandoned owing to difficulties relating to consecration and the impracticalities and logistical problems relating to the fact he died a long way from the area. Hence, upon his death at Gray's Inn Square on 29 March 1811 he was subsequently buried at St Andrew's Church, Holborn, something which undoubtedly would have severely irked him if he could have known!

There is perhaps more, however, to John Knill than meets the eye. He was indeed a customs officer and mayor of St Ives but he left the town to take a post as customs officer in the West Indies where, rumour has it, he made a small fortune. Many at the time claimed he may well have dabbled in smuggling a little himself. When he was mayor in 1767 he paid for the fitting out of a privateer, which was apparently used for smuggling. One story links Knill to a boat loaded with china that ran aground at the Hayle side of Carrack Gladden. The crew escaped, and someone removed the ship's papers since they implicated Knill and a squire from Trevetho. Roger Wearne, the customs man of the time, helped himself to some of the cargo, but as he was climbing down from the vessel, one of the locals noticed his bulging clothes, and a few well-aimed blows ensured that the china was worthless.

There are extensive views of the area of Penwith from Worvas Hill and it is claimed that Knill possibly used the monument to send signals out to sea, be it for smuggling or spying. It was John Knill's wish to be remembered by the people of St Ives and every five years on 25 July, St James's Day, a strange ritual is performed in and from the town. The first ceremony took place in 1801 and Knill was in attendance to cavort with the participants who dressed in their white ribbons and uniforms of office to dance around the mausoleum to the old Cornish 'Furry Dance' tune before singing the Old Hundredth psalm. Carried out even during the war years, this celebration had its 200th anniversary in 2001. Heading the Knill Trust was the worshipful mayor and standard of the mace, the vicar of St Ives and the customs officer, together with the

*Knill monument*

master of ceremonies and the fiddler who escorted the two widows and ten maidens (of ten years old at most) dressed in white. The bizarre congregation climb to the top or Worvas Hill to dance around the steeple observed by dozens of local townspeople.

I remember a few years ago visiting Knill monument with my wife. As we arrived we both commented on a peculiar feeling of isolation and dread and neither of us could comprehend why, as these are not feelings that either of us are prone to. I am certainly not the sort of person who regularly experiences such feelings but all I can say is that it was like there was a terrible atmosphere. We both developed headaches, almost like there was an overriding atmospheric pressure and then all of a sudden we were sure we'd heard whispered voices; yet we were absolutely alone. I personally have to confess that I had an overwhelming feeling that I was being watched. The strange thing is that I have visited this location several further times and have had absolutely no similar experience.

A man, who had no prior knowledge of my own experiences, informed me at a later date that he had been walking past the Knill monument one day and had clearly heard voices. He certainly has since considered the monument to be a very spooky place, as others also do. One psychic that I know has claimed to have visited the monument on numerous occasions and is convinced that she has spoken to the spirit of John Knill, stating he is deeply unhappy because of the fact that he was not buried here.

In September 2005, I accompanied a team of investigators from the Paranormal Research Organisation, (PRO) including a psychic, to see if we could discover anything of interest, mainly as a result of my own experiences, of which the team were not made aware of in advance. The information the team discovered was as follows:

One investigator picked up on a young boy aged about seven to eight years old; he was given the name, 'John'. This spirit apparently comes in visitation, and died as a result of an accident in 1490. It would seem that this child joined a party out hunting; he was running ahead of the group and was killed by a loose shot, which missed the prey, and accidentally killed him.

The psychic who apparently had no prior knowledge, sensed bones inside the monument, and she could also see young girls being led here. They had flowers on their heads, she felt that this may have been for some kind of ceremony they may have been given bags of money, possibly as a gift. Though her information did relate to a degree to the site I still feel overall that this was a disappointing set of results.

# Lelant

At the bottom of Lelant village there is a cottage. At this location back in the 1920s a lady had a very strange experience, which she related to me personally some years ago. The cottage had once been a police house and on one particular night the lady awoke to see a small girl leaning over her bed. The child was smiling and had long plaits in her hair. There was no reason to assume this girl wasn't real as she appeared very solid and genuine and so the lady (young girl at the time) asked 'who let you in?' at which point the little girl she had seen promptly vanished, with no obvious rational explanation for it.

In another nearby house in the same village, a young Labrador (or retriever) -type dog is said to haunt the property. People have observed it pottering around the interior of the house and also in the grounds. Sightings are usually brief but he has a habit of appearing and disappearing several times in a short period. The house is less than a century old and so it is assumed that this is a former pet from maybe a few years before.

There is also another wacky and unlikely story in the village. It is claimed that many years ago, a man was out walking when he heard the tolling bells of Lelant Church. As he approached he could see that the lights were on and the bells were still ringing, if seeming a little muffled. He glanced in through a window and to his astonishment saw a funeral possession, bathed in light, moving down the centre of the aisle. The church was crammed with people, only they were not normal people but little people and they all looked very sorrowful. He described how the mourners all carried and wore flowers and wreaths and six of them were carrying a stretcher with the body of a beautiful, tiny, female. When the men reached the altar they began to dig a hole into which the body was laid. As the remains vanished from sight the group all sang 'our queen is dead' and the men started to shovel earth into the grave. At this point the man shrieked and all of a sudden the lights vanished and the fairies allegedly attacked him. He claimed that at this point he had to flee for his life. Perhaps not a likely story but nevertheless it has been told for quite some years.

# Lelant, Club

Since the 1920s there have been ghostly events at a location in the countryside here. The building is believed to have been a former counthouse for nearby Balnoon Mine and may indeed be haunted by miners, a grieving woman and poltergeist activity. Some of the stranger events over the years have included:

- A clock, perched on a mantelpiece, seen by several witnesses to vibrate and rock from side to side, then it was seen to lift an inch or so from the mantelpiece before dropping back into place.
- Many items have gone missing, especially clothes, some of which have never returned.
- Two diners in the restaurant saw sugar containers start to shake noisily and then float across the room before hovering and then smashing onto the floor. Also a waitress in the same restaurant was once hit on her chest by, of all things, a flying lemon.
- In the bar, a pile of towels was found on the floor. A barman put them back in place and just moments later they had once again been placed on the floor and yet nobody else had been in the vicinity.
- Doors were often found to have been unlocked as if by themselves, at night, when nobody could have done this.
- Lights were frequently turned on and off by themselves and as a result many of the staff members refused to turn lights off at night due to the fear involved.
- Various personal feelings such as tingling, people's hair rising and goose pimples were all experienced and reported on a regular basis.

However there have also been several sightings in the building as well, including a man in miner's clothing believed to be a man who died in the nearby mine which runs underneath the building, and a shadowy figure of a woman witnessed in the bar area by several independent people. Others have just seen a skirt disappearing around the bar and multiple witnesses have seen the same figure in the identical place. This may be either a lady who died suspiciously with her baby upstairs or a lady who died at the end of the nineteenth century, drowning in a nearby pool.

# Ludgvan

At a crossroads between Ludgvan and St Ives there lies a site where suicide victims were buried in centuries gone by. In the 1920s, when a road was being built, they discovered and removed a coffin. The ghost of a former suicide is now said to walk this area at night.

In a cottage in the village it is also reported that every morning at 5.00 a.m. there is a banging at the front door. It is described as being very loud as if someone is in a panic trying to get people's attention. However, whenever anyone goes to the door, there is absolutely nobody there. The family didn't stay there very often and so a friend of theirs would regularly pop in to check on the place. On one of her visits she went inside and checked on the building and, after checking upstairs, she turned to go down the spiral staircase when she stopped in her tracks because she could see a figure at the bottom of the stairs. She described this man as appearing like an old-fashioned tramp and in her panic she realised that her only escape was to dash past him. Being unsure of his intentions she tried to run past him and as she got near to him, he vanished in front of her very eyes.

Other people staying in the house had other experiences and on one occasion a little girl, aged about five, was one of those staying in the abode. She told how she had been in the bedroom and had met a new friend. This was also a little girl but the odd thing was that she had no legs. It transpired that the floor had been raised by about 2ft by the then owners. So it appears this girl was standing on the original floors.

# Mitchell, nr Hayle

Back in the 1960s a lady was driving through this village on a sunny afternoon. As she continued along the road she suddenly saw a young girl, aged about eight or nine, skipping along the side of the street. She noticed her in particular because she was wearing a Victorian-style blue and white pinafore dress, with boots and stockings. Unexpectedly the girl danced out towards the road and without any warning headed out in front of a lorry. However, the vehicle didn't even break and in shock the lady looked at the road but there was absolutely no sign of any child and it appeared that the lorry driver had been oblivious to her presence.

# Nancledra

Back in 2002 I received an e-mail from a gentleman who was enquiring about a ghost he believes might haunt the village of Nancledra. On a late evening in August at about 8.00 p.m., he was travelling south along the B3311 from St Ives when he suddenly witnessed something appear on the right hand side of the road. It was as if something was approaching from the woodland there and he described a grey hooded figure, possibly a monk. This spectral form seemed to glide across in front of his car before vanishing through a stone wall on the left. The sudden appearance had made him brake very hard and he soon realised that there was a car coming the opposite way, which did exactly the same thing. Evidently this driver had seen this as well, so there were multiple witnesses, which would certainly suggest that he was not imagining anything. He looked at the other driver and in his own words 'from this and the expression on the other driver's face as we passed, I could only assume that he saw it as well'. The gentleman

*Nancledra*

concerned insists he had never previously had any paranormal experiences, so is not prone to imagination. Furthermore, when he told a local villager friend; he was informed that it was common knowledge in the area that the road was haunted by just such a figure.

I must admit that I regularly do drive on this road and on misty nights it certainly takes on a very atmospheric countenance. However, I have not witnessed anything similar. On one occasion, though, I was driving through Nancledra at about midnight when I saw a man standing against a wall. He was completely still and I was very surprised to see him there at that time of night. I looked again and he was gone and I couldn't understand how he possibly disappeared so quickly. I have no idea, however, whether this was just perhaps someone behaving erratically.

## Norway Square

The area around Norway Square, known as Downlong, stretches from Porthgwidden Beach across to the Tate and to the Market Place and is full of very old buildings and granite cottages, many of which were used in years gone by as cottages to house some of the numerous local fishermen. The streets are often described as being like a rabbit warren and are small, invariably

*Norway Square*

cobbled and as quaint as can be. Within this area, populated in the past mainly by fisher folk and their families, there is one particular 200-year-old cottage with a sinister reputation and plenty of apparent 'spiritual' activity that has been reported for over 100 years and reached a frequency in the 1970s.

Although activity had occurred previously it began again with a vengeance in the late 1970s; when a new family moved in. They had an eight-year-old girl staying at the residence and one night they awoke to discover her screaming. Her parents found her running across the landing in a state of apparent terror. She kept screaming, 'the lady wants me, the lady wants me'. Once the parents calmed her down the little girl described how this lady had appeared in her room and had actually held her in her arms. She apparently spoke to her and said that her own daughter had died and she wanted her instead. As the next few days went by she was insistent of her story's authenticity and spoke of very little else. She also refused to sleep in the bedroom but asked to sleep with her parents instead, indeed this went on for months and the poor girl became increasingly withdrawn and melancholic.

Out of desperation, the family eventually decided to call in a renowned local medium and made sure that they invited her into the house, without giving her any prior information. The psychic revealed that she felt there to be the presence of an eight-year-old girl in the house. Furthermore this child had died in the late nineteenth century as a result of contracting

*Norway Square*

cholera and the mother had suffered from terrible guilt. In essence the poor woman had been devastated at the death of her child (the eldest of four) and it is believed died later herself of what many whom knew her described as a broken heart. It was said in the weeks after her daughter's death, she had barely eaten or slept and eventually this self-neglect had taken its toll on her. Unfortunately the events described by the family living in the house at the time of the story continued for months; until eventually the girl came down one morning to say: 'the lady is going to leave me alone', apparently because she was nearly nine years old and no longer the same age as her daughter.

Another ghost, believed to be the mother, also apparently haunted the same cottage. The residents had all frequently heard footsteps outside a particular bedroom door and travelling down the stairs. This was always at the same time of night and yet nobody was ever seen. The medium, spoken of above, also commented on this presence and asked the family if they'd found anything when they moved in, because this ghost was upset at the removal of a straw cross. Apparently the family had indeed recently thrown one away and on hearing this, the family retrieved it and the footsteps abated.

Nearby there is a seated courtyard area called Norway Square and this is also linked heavily to the same story. Apparently when the Victorian family were alive the children had often played in this area and after the child's death from cholera the mother had frequently been found in this place, crying and lost in her morose thoughts for her daughter. Often people would come over to her and ask if she was all right but she would just shrug them away as if she just wanted to be left alone. Today Norway Square is well known for reported strange occurrences, which have happened in its vicinity. Firstly one may well note the fact that it is invariably empty, despite seemingly being a perfect location for people to take a seat. There have been a number of reasons put forward to explain the fact it is often vacant and these relate to numerous strange goings on. It is believed that the four children, who had lived in the nearby house, had played in this area and the mother used to often be seen, in her final days after her daughter's death, sat here reminiscing about her lost child. Many people have claimed to have negative feelings whilst being in the area and they describe unexplainable drops in temperature. For example in the middle of a sunny hot August afternoon, people have been known to shiver with the cold, despite there being no obvious rational explanation as to why. A number of people have also been here and claimed to have heard a woman's voice or a child's chuckling noise. There have also been a few sightings of a young woman, knelt or sat near the floor, crying her eyes out. She is usually described in what appears to be a long, black, Victorian mourning dress. There have even been a few people who have claimed to feel a physical sensation as if someone has pushed them (being shrugged away?). However, the most common experience reported in Norway Square is a feeling of overwhelming emotion, an almost unbearable sadness. This in itself is very interesting when you realise that most of these people have entered the area in a good mood, they are perhaps on holiday and happy. The links to the above story are evident and some claim that the mother may haunt both the house and the square.

I have often witnessed people attending my ghost walks react strongly to this area and describe many of the feelings I list above. The intriguing thing is that this is always before I tell the story and so autosuggestion would not appear to have played a part. One night I had two independent witnesses describe seeing a lady in black (in the same way as mentioned above), their descriptions were identical and yet they described these experiences to me separately. I did not unfortunately see anything personally.

# Phillack, Bucket of Blood Pub

This alarmingly titled pub near Hayle has a great deal of fascinating history and is linked to ghostly activity and a notorious legend. Nothing can be more disturbing than the myth which reputedly gives the pub its name. From early times there has been a pub here and it has previously been the supposed haven for pirates, smugglers, sailors and the like. A deep well served the inn at one time and one morning, several centuries ago, the then landlord went to raise the bucket to collect water. As he brought up the pail he brought up not water but blood. Later a search discovered a badly mutilated body at the bottom of the well and it is claimed to have been a revenue officer who was investigating the smuggling activity. Though the truth may never be known it is certainly a macabre story. The ghost stories attached to the place include ghostly figures being seen crossing the road outside, footsteps moving across the creaking floorboards upstairs and many other strange occurrences.

What better place than this for a paranormal investigation and that is exactly what happened in 2003 when I accompanied a team of fellow investigators from the Paranormal Research Organisation (PRO) on an investigation here and in the nearby graveyard. This research team comprised of a mixture of psychic and sceptics but the psychic team, who had no prior knowledge of the building, came up with the following intriguing information:

*Phillack, Bucket of Blood pub*

- A male presence who had been murdered in the cellar and who left the pub via the cellar door and crossed the road where he then went through the hedge, opposite the pub. He may well have been a previous landlord who walks across the road outside. Dowsing results revealed that he might have been called Bernard and aged in his forties. He may have been murdered.
- The presence of a young male aged between seventeen and nineteen years old was picked up, he was not linked to the pub but the land the pub stood on. This was also an area where a number of the team developed feelings of sadness and loneliness
- A smuggler's tunnel under the building, running from opposite the garage, which was formerly a stable and is about 8ft wide and 32ft deep. It appears to be separate to the pub and more likely to have been used for smuggling rather than as a mining tunnel.
- An old woman in the bar was identified and though she was unsure of her exact age she was well into her eighties. She possibly lived nearby, down the road and was linked to the area, although the team were unsure if it is the pub that links her or just the area where she was.
- A cat and a female dog were found in an outside garage perhaps linked to a former stable.
- The presence of a one-eyed man called Jack, who was a sexton and regular to the pub was discovered.

- The presence of an elderly man and woman, not regulars to the pub and linked to the landlord not the pub were identified.
- Twin nine-year-old girls were identified in the bar area.
- The smell of dead rabbits picked up in the bar by several investigators.

At the end, results were discussed with the landlord and much of the information seemed to be accurate when compared to previously known activity and history, despite as always the team not being allowed access to known information before an investigation. The most exciting discovery was probably the news that a man called Jack, who had only had one eye, used to drink here in recent years. He apparently came to the pub every night until he died in 1972. He would sit in a particular chair, this being exactly where our psychic had sensed his presence. Furthermore his photo was provided and matched the descriptions given to an absolute staggering degree of similarity! The landlord later confirmed that this man Jack had indeed been the sexton for the churchyard next door. It also seems that a former landlady, Mrs Chandler is sometimes seen, as is a landlord. Some smelt the smell of rabbits, which appeared to relate to a true fact. Two nine-year-old girls were picked up in an area where people keep asking if there is anything strange because they feel a presence. There have been sightings of a man and a lady.

In addition, afterwards several intrepid volunteers, including myself, headed off into the graveyard nearby to search for strange activities and a monk who is apparently sited here and during the visit a camera failed to work and another refused to turn off. A stone in the churchyard has been sited here for 1500 years and many people from the nearby estate have claimed that a monk is seen walking nearby. The ghostly figure was apparently seen by quite a number of witnesses, including the previously mentioned sexton Jack and dogs are often known to play up.

# Phillack, Lethlean Lane

Many years ago there were two young men walking down the road by Phillack Church when they heard the sound of approaching footsteps. The footsteps got progressively closer but nobody actually appeared. However the two men described a feeling as if a cold breeze had passed them. The fact that it was a still day led the two men to become instantly nervous and they ran towards Hayle. This is something that has been reported many times over the years in this street and always at the same spot. It is also a place where animals frequently act up. Dogs are often known to stop, begin to growl, their hackles going up and refusing point blank to carry on past the spot. Some believe that these phenomenon are related to the ghost of Canon Hockin, a previous rector of Phillack Church. He was in position there from the middle to the end of the nineteenth century and his spectre, wearing a black cloak, has allegedly been seen walking in the area on several occasions. I have also been told about a monk who walks in the area – but I assume that this is the same figure, being given different interpretations by different witnesses.

# Porthmeor, Carrack Dhu

There is an oft-quoted story that appears in many of the older local ghost books but that has also been part of spoken word of mouth for quite some time. Separate people have seen a boat containing people swathed in long robes arriving on the beach near the cliff. It appears to be a

*Porthhmeor, Carrack Dhu*

small craft, like a rowing boat. The sailors then form a group and appear to be talking frantically, yet no actual sound is ever heard. Then amazingly, the assembly start climbing up the cliff and when they reach the summit they form into a huddle and kneel down as if in prayer. At this point they are said to vanish in front of any present and startled witnesses. Anyone who has seen this over the years has been completely shocked and assumed there is obviously some kind of supernatural event taking place. There does certainly appear to be some kind of religious significance to this, according to the clothing and the actions of the collective apparition.

It is very difficult to ascertain why such an event would take place, though one possibility has been given as relating to the story of St Eia of whom the town of St Ives is allegedly given its name. Back in the fifth century, legend claims that an Irish princess came to the area and spread Christianity to the local 'heathens'. The legend tells how St Eia, a virgin saint of noble birth, went to the seashore in her native Ireland to depart for Cornwall, along with other saints. Finding that they had gone without her, fearing that she was too young for such a hazardous journey, she was grief stricken and began to pray. As she prayed she noticed a little leaf floating on the water and touched it with a rod to see if it would sink. However, as she looked it grew bigger and bigger. She decided that God had sent it to her and unquestioning she stepped upon the leaf and was straightaway wafted across the Irish Channel, reaching her destination before the others. The tale goes on to say that Eia founded an oratory in the clearing of a wood on the site of the existing parish church that is dedicated to her in modern day St Andrews Street. Interestingly, during construction of the new lifeboat station that is close to the parish church, the contractors excavated a peat bog, which is surprising when one considers the excavations were in St Ives Harbour. Some claim that the described image may be somehow related to her and the other Saints arrival, though in fact the legend maybe doesn't quite fit the reported sighting here.

# Regent Hotel

I was fortunate enough to be invited to this hotel by Keith the owner, both to hear his fascinating stories and at a later date to carry out an investigation with some of my colleagues from the PRO. Indeed the team has since returned again with different investigators for a follow-up investigation. On both occasions the team left the hotel with some intriguing results.

In terms of history, the hotel and building next door used to be one large house, much of which was added on later. It was used both as a sea captain's house and it was also owned by a mine superintendent who used the building as his town house, with his main residence at Halsetown. Then, in the Second World War, American forces commandeered the building for use under the command of General Bradley, in preparation for Operation Overlord. A large number of servicemen from the 29th U.S. Rangers and the 34th U.S. Infantry stayed here at the hotel and left for France from nearby Trebah Beach, to take part in the Normandy landings. Sadly many of them died during the operations and so the Regent Hotel would have been their last known place for peace and safety before the shock and trauma of what was to come.

There are several ghosts that are said to haunt this hotel. Several witnesses have seen a respectable, well-to-do gentleman. They have all described him as being small in stature, elderly and wearing nineteenth-century clothing. Similarly guests and staff alike have seen him and there was one particular chambermaid who worked here in the past who claimed that she had seen him on a regular basis and indeed became, in her own words, quite fond of him. The majority of sightings have occurred in a particular bedroom but also in the outdoor corridor and on the main staircase. He is suspected to be the former mine superintendent who would have worked in the building when this was actually a count house. His appearances become apparently more frequent during times of work or renovation at the hotel.

At the foot of the staircase, people have seen a man in a long frock coat. He is described as being well built and is often seen to be smiling. On one occasion a guest said good morning to him, at which point he disappeared. Some people have said the coat is of a military-style grey and so could well fit in with the former wartime usage of the premises.

On the first floor there is a frequently described phenomenon that occurs where people hear a sound as though someone knocking on the doors. This has also been known to happen, at the same time, in the building next door and the relevant corridors were indeed known to have interconnected when the buildings were all in one.

Years ago a swimming pool was being built and two builders, described as 'hefty fellas', stayed at the hotel in a twin room. They both claimed to have seen a ghost in the room and were visibly shocked by this experience. In fact they were so upset that they demanded to move rooms and

*Regent Hotel*

stated they would even prefer to stay together in a double bed rather than reside another night in this particular room.

In Room One, people were once filming with a camcorder when a ghostly figure appeared behind them in the room on the screen but unfortunately no copy of this is available for inspection. In the same room a couple were staying a few years ago when they woke to find that a heavy bedside table had been moved. When they went to move it back, they could hardly lift it.

There is also a room on the top floor leading to a roof space, which has been a source for a lot of activity over the last few years. Most people feel quite uncomfortable here and it is believed to be the ghost of a former maid. One former chambermaid became quite attached to her and described her as friendly. One guest also described seeing a lady in a mobcap, wearing a black skirt. She was seen in the outside corridor and disappeared though the wall, leading to next door.

Talking of the next-door building, a figure has also been seen in there in several separate places, and the area is described as a cold and mysterious place. Intriguingly this figure is similarly described as walking down a corridor in that building and then going through the wall leading to the Regent Hotel. A stable boy also allegedly haunts the hotel building and it turns out that at the time when the buildings were a mine superintendent's, this part was in fact the stables.

Things in general do get more pronounced at times of renovation. Often the hotel is subject to crashing and banging noises, poltergeist movements, lights found blazing in empty rooms; indeed the electricity bill does tend to go up in the hotel during times of such renovation.

In summary, then, the building itself was a large house belonging to a sea captain, named Chellew and built by James Halse. It has been owned by the present owners for about thirty years. In the Second World War, the US 29th Rangers and 134th Infantry stayed here before Operation Overlord under the command of General Bradley who used it as a general headquarters:

- A 'well-to-do' man has been seen in a bedroom, the corridors and on the main staircase – he may have been a former mine superintendent and dresses in smart clothes from the nineteenth century. He is small and elderly.
- At the bottom of the stairs – an older man is seen in a long frock coat. He is well built and dressed possibly in an American military uniform.
- First Floor – the doors are often knocked as if someone is going from room to room (here and then in the next building – they used to be the same large house).
- Room Eight (twin room) – several sightings have been made here.
- Room One – furniture is often moved – particularly a small cabinet. People also claim to have caught a figure on film.
- It is said to be particularly active during renovations – lights, electrics play up.
- A chambermaid may haunt the top floor – things move and many people find it uncomfortable.

During the first PRO investigation I personally researched the place in advance and so when I attended I was armed with a reasonable amount of prior knowledge. Nevertheless, as is standard practice to avoid any contamination of evidence or autosuggestion, I purposefully kept this data to myself and gave nothing away until after the team had investigated and particularly after the psychic had already dowsed for information.

The investigation began with a brief tour of the hotel with Keith the owner. He was specifically asked to withhold all information at this stage, though one investigator felt a strong presence at the bottom of the stairs.

## Room Eight:

Two investigators dowsed and picked up on a female presence named Elizabeth, who was associated with the building and who was aged forty-five at the time of her death in around 1928. This may have been in an accident, possibly a fire in the building, which killed three people.

They also identified a male presence, which may have been Elizabeth's husband. He visited but did not live here and died in the 1930s from a heart attack in America, aged sixty-six. He has been seen in this room but also moves to other places. Information also suggested he was American, travelled, was a professional and well known and that he worked with money and was linked to the military.

Some of the information seemed to link with both the American serviceman seen and the mine superintendent, perhaps information was becoming confused between the two?

Finally the team came up with a female, who had been aged in her fifties and who died in 1968. She may have been the daughter of the other presences.

## Room One:

Varying temperatures were taken across the room between 11°c and 18°c during the investigation in and then the same two investigators began to dowse for information.

Firstly they found a strong male presence that was friendly and who had died aged eighteen but had not lived or indeed died here. He had passed away in 1944 in an explosion linked to the war. His name was Robert Lamberg and he was of Jewish descent. He had been American and had a girlfriend back home and he was sad and missed her and his family. The investigators suggested that he tries to bring attention to himself by moving things in this room and playing with the television. Knowing that the cabinet in this room has supposedly been moved on occasions, I asked an investigator if he could find out what the presence moves and he came up with the kettle and, remarkably, the cabinet.

The team then identified a second male aged nineteen and named Bud. It turned out that this had been a nickname and him and Robert had been friends and in service together, in fact they had been roommates. Bud had apparently been shot dead in the Second World War after Robert had died.

A third presence made a brief and sudden intrusion and came in from the door and then left before any real information could be found. One investigator asked Robert and Bud and revealed that this was their commanding officer entering and checking on them.

A strong knocking was heard coming from a wardrobe and when we checked it there was no obvious explanation for the cause. This happened five times in here and there were also knocking sounds emanating from the door. We attempted to rationalise these sounds but were unable to do so.

As a first for the PRO the team decided at midnight to hold a séance in Room One and this proved to be very eventful and interesting, as peculiar lights were seen and a shadow or figure seen near the door. Two investigators both felt they could see a presence and another felt prodded in his back, whilst yet another came over very peculiar, with feelings of pins and needles. At one stage an investigator went off alone to the toilet and heard a distinctive knocking which she couldn't explain.

## Room Seven:

At 11.30 the team gathered in this room and one investigator began to dowse for information and picked up on a male aged forty-six who had died in 1886. He had lived here and worked in service for James Halse as a butler. This had apparently been his room but he had not died in the building. He had purportedly died in an accident, being crushed when he was run over outside the hotel by a horse and cart delivering coal. He had been married and had one child who had lived here too. His wife turned out to have worked here as a maid and was said to be the 'phantom knocker' described elsewhere. Results showed that his name was Francis and suddenly the dowsing rods suggested that he had left through the door. We followed the path indicated by the rods, only to see them stop at each door in turn in the order of rooms: Two, Three, Five, and Six before going back to room Seven. Once inside here again we found out that he apparently locks and unlocks doors, as he would have done for his job.

At the end of the investigation, the team took a break in the hotel lounge and began to chat with the owner Keith about how the information about Rooms One and Eight compared to his own knowledge. He confirmed much of the information to be accurate and his wife also said that the kettle in Room One often turned on by itself. In Room Eight a suitcase had also flown off a wardrobe and thuds and knockings have regularly been heard. The first-floor rooms also often get unlocked at night without explanation. So this seemed to have been a very good start in terms of findings.

Overall this was an intriguing and thought-provoking night, with quite a few things being picked up that seemingly related to previously known activity. As a result another independent team returned over eighteen months later to see what they could find. Once again results and previous activity were kept from them and this time we had a much larger team. The team began the second investigation in three groups, focusing on the hotel to begin with, before moving into another building at approximately 2.00 a.m.

## Investigation Findings – Investigation Two

### Lounge:

The team photographed many light anomalies in the lounge doorway and around one of the psychic team during the vigil.

The team that investigated this room used dowsing rods and found one male presence that they identified as sitting in the chair by the radiator with the possible name of Gilbert. He was a past resident of the building when it was a house and died at the age of ninety-six, this apparently being in the property back in the 1820s. They also found that he had been married but that his wife's spirit was not present in the building.

The second presence detected was that of a female, located in another nearby chair. Dowsing revealed the possible name of Claire Filbert and that she died aged seventy-five, in the year 1830. She was also a past resident of the house. She was later detected in another part of the room, suggesting she had moved around.

### Dining/Breakfast room:

On entering this, the next investigation area, the electro magnetic frequency (EMF) meter was reading 6mg in the doorway to the hall and 3-4mg in the middle of the room. Thirty to forty seconds later all readings had disappeared. The same team as had investigated the lounge area, dowsed and found a male presence, near the doorway to the kitchen. They identified a potential name of George and that he had been a thief, sailor, smuggler and possibly murderer, being caught for his crimes and hung. He was never a resident, guest or employee of the building, so it was not evident why his spirit was there. During this time several investigators felt a definite cold spot near the archway to the kitchen. There were no obvious draughts and there was a radiator just next to the spot. This was the area where investigators had detected the presence of George.

The next team to investigate this area also used the art of dowsing to find a female presence. This particular spirit was seemingly aware that she had passed, this being in 1968 at the age of sixty-five. She worked here during the Second World War as a clerk and the team felt that she was happy here and had died somewhere in England, though not Cornwall.

The next presence to be identified by this team was a male next to the door by the bathroom. He died in France in 1944, during the Second World War and comes in visitation because he liked the place and his friends are with him here.

A second male was then revealed, who also died in 1944 during the Normandy landings after being stationed at the hotel in the previous five months.

A third male then came to light and who had died of natural causes, this being cholera. The initial J was identified and that he was linked to a certain James Halse who had built a small village not too far away.

Before the third and final team began to investigate this particular room, one of their investigators reported that she had felt the presence of three males who walked from the lounge towards the kitchen.

Dowsing from an independent investigator in this area revealed three males. The first male was by the door and gave the name George. He had been married, had worked there and had died from a heart attack in the year 1834. The second male, named Henry had been a chef before dying in 1933 from heart problems. The third male had the name Robert and was directly in front of one of the investigators. This person then asked for a sign and a slight draught was felt over their right hand. The team established that Robert was an American soldier, who had been training here for the Normandy Invasion in 1944. He had sadly been killed in action during the assault. During this part of the investigation; team members heard several thuds and one investigator reported that she was drawn to the window, where she felt that an ancient battle had been fought.

## Room One:

The first team to investigate this room picked up on two presences, one being male and the other female, though they were not related to one another.

The other team to investigate this location reported hearing laughter as they entered the area. They also revealed that two energy lines crossed the room. The only presence detected in here by this team was that of a male presence who apparently comes in visitation.

## Room Two:

One team investigated this room and found four presences all of which were male and from the same time span and that they knew each other. They had all been Irish servicemen ranked as privates in the light infantry and sadly they all had died in action in 1942. They had been stationed in this building before going to war.

## Room Three:

The team to investigate this room picked up on a single male presence sitting on the bed. Investigators felt that he had never lived here and indeed had not died in the premises. He may have been of African descent and possibly had the name Lija. Furthermore, dowsing identified that he had been a sailor who'd worked on a ship called *Franciscane Gem*.

## Room Six:

The first team to investigate this room picked up on one male presence, an army officer in the Second World War. It was felt that he comes back to this room because he liked it here. The investigators identified the name Albert and that he died abroad during the war. The presence conveyed at this stage that he had whispered in an investigator's ear whilst that person had been in the corridor. When the team later checked this, they discovered that a researcher had in fact heard whispering in his ear in the described place. This would appear to have been a very peculiar occurrence or a remarkable coincidence.

The second team did not feel at all comfortable whilst they were in this room. In contrast though, they identified a female who had not died of natural causes. In 1885 a man allegedly suffocated this young lady who at the time had been aged twenty-three. Nevertheless she had not been murdered in this building but had known her killer and had been killed because of a relationship she had been having with someone.

## Room Seven:

The team investigating this room revealed a petite female named Christine. Dowsing also showed that she had been thirty-three years old at the time of her death in 1841. She had worked here as a chambermaid and her spirit was apparently looking out of the window. This unfortunate lady had been murdered, possibly by being smothered or strangled and one particular investigator actually reported feeling a restriction around her throat.

## Room Eight:

Very high EMF readings were recorded in the middle of this room between the two twin beds, where a vortex had apparently been discovered by one of the investigators. The readings stopped and started and were taken in mid-air with no obvious wiring-related cause or other reason being found for this. An investigator instantly felt something had happened in this room and the whole team all noticed a peculiar smell and feelings of dizziness and gloom. Three of the investigators had to leave the room and couldn't stay for any longer than five minutes.

The presence of a child named Jenny was identified near the headboard of one of the beds and at the same time, the EMF meter registered 5mg in this same area. This child was described as a female of six years old who back in 1850 had been strangled or suffocated by a woman, in this very room. There appeared to be a second presence in the room who was frightening Jenny and therefore preventing her from telling the team who had murdered her.

Whilst the team had been in this room, one of them had heard someone knocking on the bedroom door. On investigating there was no one in the corridor and intriguingly another team, positioned directly above, had also heard a knocking noise at exactly the same time. They called down to ask if anyone had been upstairs but all investigators were accounted for and the knocking noise therefore remains a mystery.

The team all felt much better on leaving the room and believed that guests staying in that room must have felt something in there.

## Room Nine:

The first team to investigate this room uncovered a male presence who had died of natural causes. He was standing next to the window area and was not happy possibly because he had suffered from Parkinson's disease. The team got the name Charles and that he had once been in the British army, mentioning a date of 1945.

The second team to investigate this room brought to light the presence of a small boy and immediately the team recorded a small drop in temperature.

One investigator got the feeling that the small boy had dark hair and that he was of slight build. Another felt quite emotional at a time when cold spot were also being picked up in the area where this boy apparently was. The team tried reciting nursery rhymes in order to get some kind of response, and they all heard a small unexplainable bang.

## Room Ten:

The first team to investigate this room found there to be three presences; a husband and wife and a further male. The female was next to the door and it seems that she had been murdered by strangulation in 1684, by the male presence in the room that was not her husband. He had killed her because she had something in her possession, acquired through smuggling, that was not hers and he had murdered her for it.

Her Cornish husband may have been called Jacob Henderson and had been a sailor; he felt responsible for the murder because he had given the item to his wife. He killed the other man in retribution and later died in Spain.

The second team to investigate this room revealed that there was a male presence called Sidney in the bathroom. They concluded that this was a military man, possibly a captain during the Second World War who died at the age of forty-eight in 1949.

*First-Floor Landing area:*
The team found a single presence at the top of the stairs, a female named Eleanor. She had died in the building when she was fifty years old and this was due to natural causes, maybe an illness.

*Top-Floor Corridor:*
The team in this locality identified two male presences. One was a male sailor who had been both single and local. The presence gave a date of 1842 and that he had died as the result of a heart attack in room five which had been his bedroom.

Overall, the second investigation team had picked up on a great deal of information, some of which appeared relevant to previously reported activity but also similar to findings of the first team.

# Richmond Lane

Running adjacent to the Barbara Hepworth Museum and Sculpture Garden is a back lane leading into Richmond Place. It has become notorious in recent years within the local area for possibly being the most actively haunted place in St Ives and there is regularly reported activity. What has always impressed me about this particular location is that the numerous sightings and other activities have been of a remarkably consistent nature. It is of course almost impossible to ascertain that any haunted location is definitively haunted but of course the more frequently the same thing is experienced by people with no prior knowledge of the story the better chance that it might be authentic – that is certainly the case with this example.

The vision that has been witnessed here is that of a white figure. Invariably it occurs between 11 p.m. and midnight. People have walked around the bottom corner and have begun to meander up the incline of the hill. They then suddenly see a figure appearing around the top corner, swathed all in white. Indeed it is as if the figure is wearing a long, flowing white garment. People's instant reaction is usually one of astonishment, as this person doesn't look quite right, although it should be said that it does look solid and real. Some people have reported an almost animal-like instinctual feeling of dread and feeling all the hairs standing up on the backs of their neck. People usually continue to stare at the figure and the whole time she (as they do assume the presence is female) moves steadily closer and closer towards them. It is then described how when she gets to within a few metres she suddenly just vanishes, right in front of their very eyes; something, which undoubtedly comes as quite a shock to them. However, witnesses seem unable to give any realistic description or recount whether it is definitely female or male, apart from the assumption based on the long, flowing garment.

Unfortunately there is no definitive answer as to who this alleged ghost might actually be, although naturally enough with such a well-known story, as this has become, there has been quite a lot of debate and discussion into the possibilities. One person who many believe the ghost might be is Barbara Hepworth, the well-known artist who died in a fire in the nearby museum in 1975. She is claimed to have been one of Britain's most important twentieth-century artists, producing renowned sculptures in bronze, stone and wood. Many of these items are now on display in the nearby museum and garden, along with paintings, drawings and archive material. It was her wish to establish her home and studio as a museum of her work, Trewyn Studio and much of the artist's work remaining there was given to the nation and placed in the care of the Tate Gallery in 1980. However my own personal opinion is that the figure seen in

*Richmond Lane*

the lane is not her ghost, as if she was to haunt anywhere, surely it would be far more likely to be the museum itself rather than a dark back lane.

There is also the chance that because this is a well-known ghost story, people are jumping to conclusions. After all when you get a frequently discussed 'ghost' right next to where someone famous lived and died, well there is certainly a tendency for people to make such assumptions.

The other candidate, who might be considered as a possibility to be the ghostly figure, is a local lady who died in nearby Richmond Lane just over twenty years ago. Unfortunately, in her final weeks she had become very unwell and had been suffering from the effects of senile dementia. As a result her behaviour had become more and more erratic and she carried out some very strange things. For example, she would often sneak out of the house late at night, something her family were completely oblivious to as they had earlier put her to bed. Then, dressed in her long, flowing white nightdress, she would wander down Richmond Lane and then turn the bottom corner and head into the town centre of St Ives, where she would meander through the main streets. Naturally, as she was dressed in her nightdress this caused quite an amount of hilarity and has thus been well remembered. Eventually though, people actually informed her family who were surprised and embarrassed but who nevertheless kept a closer eye on her and the night-time wanderings ceased. Evidently the fact that she used to walk down the lane late at night, dressed in such a manner, appears to strongly match the descriptions of the ghostly figure. Also, although there have been many reported sightings of such a white figure, all of them have occurred over the last twenty years, so naturally she does have to be a strong candidate. Furthermore I have known several mediums or psychics, who over the years have spoken of a name for the supposed ghost and, uncannily, they have mentioned the name of the elderly lady who died, despite not having this information beforehand. They have been able to mention both first and surname and yet this is not something easily researched.

Another occurence that happens in this lane is the sound of ethereal footsteps. People have often been in the lane late at night when they have heard the clear sound of footsteps, as though someone was about to walk around the top corner of the lane. Nevertheless witnesses relate the fact that nobody appears and that these footsteps carry on eerily past them and around the bottom corner, yet nobody appears to be seen.

There is also a particular spot in the lane, by the adjacent wall, where people have felt the uncanny feeling as though somebody has placed a hand on their shoulder. The spot is marked by a white square sticker (at the time of writing) so is easily found. This has happened frequently during ghost walks and I always make sure not to mention, in advance of telling the story, where the spot is and in the dark it is not easily identifiable. Nevertheless when it occurs it is always at the same spot and we can seemingly rule out autosuggestion or 'ghost-walk hype'. It is certainly very peculiar that it happens at exactly the same place and I find it hard to explain; though of course the reason behind the occurrence is unclear.

# St Erth

Centred in St Erth is a bizarre story about a nun who was apparently forbidden, when alive, to ride a horse. She is now said to ride a headless horse through the village, perhaps revelling in being allowed, now in death, to do so. It is not clear, as is so often the case in such stories, why the horse is actually headless.

# St Erth, Farmhouse

A collie dog is said to haunt a particular old dwelling here in this village on the main A30 road. The canine is most often seen going up the stairs of the house but the funny thing is that a recent farmer did in fact own a collie who detested going upstairs, mainly because he had a phobia about being given a bath. However one day the farmer was surprised to see what he thought was his dog heading up the stairs but was even more surprised to enter the kitchen and find his collie sitting under the table. It clearly had not been his dog and on closer inspection there was certainly no dog upstairs either.

# St Erth, Road

On a bendy road in the village there have been sightings of a supposed phantom car. People usually describe turning the corner and being faced by a car with headlights on full beam and being driven very fast. As the car comes round the corner it usually enters over onto the other side of the road before skidding across to the hedge opposite and hitting a tree head on. Some have claimed it then rolls over and bursts into flames, however within seconds there is absolutely no evidence remaining of the car and no sign of any accident. As people think back they realise that they had not actually heard a single sound while the car was in view. Apparently there was a terrible accident here some years ago when two women died in a way described as very similar to the incidents above.

I have not been able to verify this story but I must confess that one night I was driving through St Erth quite late when I saw a car in my mirror. The car's headlights were blazing but then in an instant it was gone. I stopped and inspected the road and there was nowhere for a car to have turned off or to have disappeared in such a short space of time. It may not have been an exact replica of the story; but nevertheless it was something I found hard to explain at the time.

## St Erth, Trewinnard Lane

There used to be a manor house at the end of this lane and a story claims that the lord of the manor's daughter used to sneak out of the house in order to visit her lover. As is so often the case in such ghost stories, the lord disapproved of the lover and of the relationship. One night, while the lady was on the way to meet her treasured sweetheart, she was murdered in the lane. Ever since people have apparently seen the ghost of a young lady in Trewinnard Lane and other people have been known to hear horse's hoof beats as if someone is riding down the lane. Occasionally people have seen a man riding the horse and this is believed to be the girl's lover.

## St Eia Church

In St Andrews Street is the parish church of St Ives. The building is dedicated to St Eia who was claimed to have been an Irish missionary who sailed to St Ives in the fifth or sixth century on a leaf (see story of Porthmeor, Carrack Dhu) and founded the original chapel. There is evidence that this site has been a place of Christian worship for over 1,500 years but the modern church was completed in 1434 and had taken twenty-four years to construct. The tower is 80ft high and made from large Cornish granite stonework, apparently shipped in from Zennor and possibly adapted from an earlier church. In the churchyard just south of the tower is a weathered fifteenth-century cross with a carving of God the Father upholding the crucified Christ. The Church of St Eia has a north aisle, south aisle and a fourth aisle on the north called the Fisherman's Aisle. It has plain glass windows designed to enable the fishermen to keep an eye on their boats in the harbour while they were in church. At the back of the Fishermen's Aisle is the baptistery, with a fifteenth-century granite font. Figurative carvings on the pedestal represent the demons cast out by baptism. The baptistery itself is mostly twentieth century, with a chequered pavement made in 1956. The choir stalls have fifteenth-century panels carved with charming human figures, which may have originally been part of the rood screen. The fine bench ends are typical of fifteenth-century Cornish woodwork with deep cutting.

On the side of the wall of the church building are several ugly faces, gargoyles and grotesques. These were carved here in the fifteenth century and legend has claimed that these are people turned to stone. Even more bizarrely is the local claim that people in the past have seen these

*St Eia Church*

gargoyles moving around on the wall and pulling funny faces at people. I am not remotely convinced that this is genuine, however, there are several mentions of this in historical texts and books published in the 1960s. I can only hope that over-indulgence of various illegal substances, in times of excessive endeavour, is not a cause for the formation of such described visions.

# St Ives Bay

There are innumerable stories concerning shipwrecks off the rugged Cornish Coast and sinister wrecks litter the coastline. With an abundance of such trauma there are also many tales about phantom ships – often witnessed floating out of a tempestuous sea and disappearing in front of startled witnesses. It is consistent in Cornwall that these ships are often heralded as harbingers of doom, vessels that are portentous, warning of impending disaster or coming storm, or of ships to be lost at sea.

One particularly well-known phantom tall ship has sporadically been seen heading across the bay at St Ives with distress flares firing. On being approached it allegedly disappears and all of a sudden. This is supposedly a ship named *The Neptune* that sank at the same place back in the nineteenth century. Richard Grant captained the boat and it is his ghost who it is claimed is trying to sail the ghostly vessel to safety, something he failed to do on its fated journey. The ghostly vessel is sometimes known as the 'Death Ship' because it is said to appear as a prelude to a forthcoming tragedy. Some years ago a fishing boat is said to have headed out to such a described ship in apparent distress. When they approached they claimed that the ship was coated in ice and when they called out to it and attempted to hail the crew, received no reply. The fishing boat's bowman leant across to grab at the other ship's bulwarks but was amazed to find his hands grasping at thin air and his fellow crewman had to grab him to stop him falling overboard. A few hours later a tempest wrecked a ship off nearby Gwithian and it appeared that the icy ship had foretold their doom.

On another occasion a local story claims that a ship was seen in distress out in the bay and a local ship headed out to assist. As they drew level with the troubled ship, they were aghast to observe it disappear in front of their very eyes.

On a further occasion another St Ives fishing crew drew alongside the phantom vessel and floated beside for some time. They even saw several ghostly figures milling around on the deck. They were nevertheless absolutely horrified when the whole spectacle vanished.

*St Ives Bay*

There may also be another similar phantom vessel seen drifting from behind the island and into the bay. Again this is an old-fashioned tall ship with grand sails. This one drifts across the bay before vanishing, again at the site of where a shipwreck may have occurred in the nineteenth century.

Many of the sailors from St Ives have also traditionally believed in the phenomenon known as 'Jack Harry's Lights'. These peculiar, dancing lights are usually said to appear as a precedent to disaster at sea. Often they would be seen over the bay dancing around a spectral ship. The description of the ship (always different) almost always matched a ship that would later fall victim to a storm and be wrecked. Often other ship's crews have mistaken them for real ships and have taken chase, only to find the mysterious vessel disappear.

Phantom bells also apparently haunt the bay. A peculiar echoing chime akin to church bells is reported to be heard coming from the middle of the sea, sounding out its peculiar carillon-esque peal. Some in the past have even suggested that perhaps there was once a lost land under the bay and these sounds are the echoes of a church from times long past. It is a famous story, but probably not genuine. For example there are lots of noises heard from out at sea, which could offer an explanation for misinterpreted sounds – such as, buoys and so on and my suspicions are that the real explanation lies therein.

# Salubrious Terrace/Virgin Street

The quaintly and uniquely named Salubrious Terrace leads on from Virgin Street and the cobbled streets have more than their fair share of attached ghost stories. In essence it is one street in all but two names, so for convenience I will refer to stories from both streets within this section.

The first story is one that I am quite convinced is as likely to be genuine as any ghost story I know due to the nature of how I learned about this account. A few years ago a young lady on a ghost walk imparted a personal experience about this street. She was walking down the lane one night, heading down from Barnoon car park, when she saw an oddly attired lady standing on the steps in front of her. She described how this woman appeared to be wearing a long black dress of Victorian appearance. She immediately sensed that there was something 'not quite right' about this figure and as she looked the lady began to slowly walk away from her down the cobbled street. She tentatively followed at a distance behind and after a few moments the figure vanished. When the lady told me this story I had genuinely not heard about such an encounter or anything strange related to this part of the street and so made a few notes and left it at that. Then a few months later I was stunned to hear of an almost identical experience and once more this was from the first-hand perspective and the descriptions were stunningly consistent. Over the last few years I have now been given first hand accounts from eight other persons who all have given me detailed and closely related accounts of the same ghostly figure. The intriguing thing is that this story is not known and is nowhere on public record. Indeed apart from the occasions when people have told me of their own experiences, I have never heard the stories. To me it is difficult to ascertain how so many independent witnesses could describe the same thing, in such a similar fashion, unless perhaps they had indeed seen exactly the same image?

In the lower part of the street, where the two streets meet, there is another story about a ghostly fireman. Apparently in the 1920s there was a fire in one of the buildings here and the story goes that a young fireman went into the building and it collapsed and he tragically died.

*Salubrious Terrace*

In recent years I am aware of a number of relevant sightings where people have been walking along the street when they have seen a man standing near the current houses wearing a fireman's uniform. Naturally people are surprised, especially as it appears to be an old-fashioned uniform. They walk past and are then drawn back to take another look only to find he has disappeared. Only recently I had some people on a ghost walk who had apparently seen this gentleman a few years back. They had actually assumed he was dressed as a fireman to collect for charity and were surprised as to where he was standing, away from the main street. They had not had any idea of this story until I told them.

There is also a building in the street where it is claimed that during the 1960s, during some renovation work, a skeleton was unearthed when an internal wall was knocked down. This caused quite some consternation because there had been many sightings over the years of a ghostly figure by that wall, something which has apparently continued since.

In one of the holiday cottages here is yet another story. A lady who works for the letting agency, who leases the property, told me that on several occasions people had come into the office to deposit the keys when they had looked at her in a strange way and asked her if the cottage was haunted. They then recount what has happened to them and invariably they have awoken to find a man standing at the bottom of their bed. He is dressed in what looks like dirty clothes and Wellington boots, a lot like a gardener but old fashioned. As it turns out the head gardener in St Ives once owned the house and he died in that very room from a heart attack!

Finally there is also another building nearby that is claimed to have been where the last person to be hung in St Ives lived. The claim is that he also haunts the building – although it is not evident what he looks like or what he actually does in terms of haunting activities.

# Skidden Hill

This street leads up from the seafront and beaches; coming down from the railway and bus stations and used to be part of the main route into St Ives. It is said that the name came from a time when carts would skid down the hill and where coaches were 'skidden down'. It is also said to be one of St Ives many haunted streets, with several different stories. For example there is a cottage in the street, which used to be a doctor's surgery and it is indeed a male doctor who is said to haunt the building.

However, it is the street itself that lays claim to the most reoccurring ghost stories. Back in the mid-to-late nineteenth century, there was a common doss house situated here and known as The Beggar's Roost. Tramps, travellers, beggars, vagrants and drunks stayed here and often hung around in this street. The building was eventually knocked down over 100 years ago but it appears that some of its residents may still be hanging around, long after their deaths.

In general what is seen here is a man or men dressed in very old fashioned, scruffy clothes. People will see one or more of them and then look away, but by the time they turn around they have disappeared, this being often just a split second later. There are two particularly consistent sightings in two different parts of the street, though of a similar basis.

The first is seen near a side wall and people are often walking along the street when they see a young man lying still and prone on the floor. He is described as wearing very poor and wretched looking clothes and people are instantly concerned at his appearance and the fact that he is lying on the ground. They feel that they should really go and see if he is ok but because of his appearance and the fact they are worrying what reaction they might get, they often turn to walk away. Nonetheless, people have then often turned back realising they should try to assist

*Skidden Hill*

him but by the time they turn around he has vanished! This has happened quite a number of times over the years.

The second story is of a young man of a similar appearance, but seen slightly further down the hill. Indeed this particular apparition is seen on a much more regular basis. He is described as also a young man in distressed and tattered clothing, though persons who have seen this particular figure say that he stands in the road with his hand outstretched as if he is begging.

There also appears to be a hat lying on the floor in front of his feet, assumely to collect money in. Once again it has often been known for people to walk past and turn around only to find that he has gone. However, the most famous example of a sighting referring to this apparition is something that happened just a few years ago. One evening at about 9.00 p.m. a young man was walking up Skidden Hill when he saw what has already been described. Due to the way this figure appeared, the young man began to feel somewhat unnerved and didn't know quite what to expect; it was getting dark, he was alone and there was this strange-looking chap hanging around. He assumed from his appearance that he was a beggar and so decided that the best thing to do would be to give the guy a few coins to keep him happy. So he put his hands into his pocket and pulled out some loose change and walked over to the 'beggar', thus depositing the coins into his hat. The beggar did not react or respond in any way and so the young man began walking up the hill in the direction in which he had been heading originally. Conversely, he had only taken a pace or two when he couldn't resist a quick glance over his shoulder and to his utter horror discovered that the beggar had disappeared in what must have been almost a split-second. The man was dumbstruck because he knew instantly that there was no way this man could have disappeared. Upon further inspection he noticed the coins lying there on the floor where the hat had previously lain. There is no question that this man could have taken these coins from the hat and placed them back on the floor without making a sound and still get out of sight by the time the young man had turned back. I am also not aware of too many beggars who have the tendency to leave coins behind. Furthermore the young man who saw this is still adamant to this day that he believes he saw a ghost that night and especially when he heard the history relating to the Beggars Roost and of the accounts relating to previous sightings here. Of course he had no prior knowledge of any of this before the episode took place. Again, if he'd been the only one ever to see this, maybe you would have to remain sceptical, but in actual fact a lot of similar sightings have occurred here. I do have to be honest though and say that I am not aware of anyone else actually putting money into this 'man's' hat!

As well as the sightings in Skidden Hill there have been a large catalogue of other strange goings on in the street including atmospheres, feelings, sounds, touches, electrical problems, pets playing up whilst in the area and other peculiar phenomena.

# Skidden House Hotel

This strategically placed and picturesque hotel was probably built in the mid-sixteenth century, which would almost certainly make it the oldest hotel in the town. It was originally constructed as a coaching inn, which served visitors heading into the town, on what was once the main coaching route into St Ives. Originally there would have been enough room for a full herd of horses to be tethered to coaches and wagons alongside the building. Throughout the history of the hotel it must have been the location for many events and there have indeed been quite a number of reported uses and different notorious owners.

Back in the seventeenth century when Oliver Cromwell's army invaded the Isles of Scilly, the Royalist prisoners of war were deposited here for a brief period of time. It is also claimed that not too many years later the hotel was used as a famous inn of ill repute where 'ladies carrying out the oldest profession in the world' plied their trade. This may have continued for some 200 or more years until the licence was taken away from the premises when the landlady of the time was discovered selling smuggled brandy and rum to Navy sailors. Also the Skidden House Hotel is said to have been the first place in the UK to serve Guinness, a claim which I personally feel is a very plaudit-worthy one indeed, the 'black stuff' being a favourite tipple of mine. In the late-eighteenth century the owner, a certain Captain Sampson, regularly sailed between the Emerald Isles and St Ives on his lugger, transporting fish and potatoes. In Dublin he became very good friends with Arthur Guinness and often sampled his new brand of porter (or stout). Naturally enough he became incredibly fond of the beverage and eventually agreed to import some and started serving it at the Skidden House Hotel.

The premises is allegedly haunted by a woman who some say is dressed in blue and others white. I was told a story years ago that claimed a lady in a long, flowing white dress was often observed gliding down the staircase and disappearing in front of a number of different residents. Many believed it was either a former chambermaid or a prostitute from the time when it was used as a brothel. Nevertheless, in more recent years the hotel's website stated:

*Skidden House Hotel*

The Skidden House Hotel is haunted by the ghost of a Lady in Blue who walks past the kitchen, through the dining room and into the reception area and has been seen by many guests before dinner, appearing to be leading them into the Restaurant. This Lady in Blue is always seen by new apprentice chefs and kitchen staff during their first few days and always before being told of the legend.

The hotel is also allegedly haunted by the ghost of a gentleman of some age, with a grey beard and seen wearing a long frock coat. This ghostly gentleman is nearly always seen on the first floor of the hotel, but seems to be unaware of the fact that the hotel has been separated into two parts, this because he moves through the wall between the hotel and the adjoining cottage. In general the ghosts are reportedly benign characters, even though they can be mischievous at times. Activity always increases when workmen are making alterations to the hotel and these goings-on have included tools disappearing only to reappear in rooms where no work is being carried out.

I used to know a previous owner reasonably well and he was adamant that the place was haunted, often encouraging me to spread the word amongst 'ghost-walkers'. However, I must confess that

I do not know the current owners and so am not aware of whether activity is still continuing at present on such a regular basis, though the hotel has always been described as bringing with it only feelings of peace and tranquillity, whether haunted or not.

# Solicitor's Building

In the town there is a building that was investigated by the PRO with some interesting results:

### Library Room in Basement:
The first team identified a male presence by the name of Frank Nicols who was a local architect and did not want the team being there, as it was his room. He was described as having a beard and sideburns and indeed one of the clean-shaven investigators actually felt this on his own face.

Another male presence who may have had the surname Ward and who used to live in the building was also detected. He may have been a sea captain or had a possible naval connection.

The second team's dowsing results incredibly revealed a male of an almost identical name, this being Frank Nicholls and they also found that he was not happy about the team being in the room, because it was his house.

### Red Room in Basement:
In this room, the team picked up on one male presence with the possible name of Callender who was standing by the desk. He had not been resident in the building but had worked there in the 1800s. He had also once held high office in the Merchant Navy and worked for a shipping company, maybe something to do with the exporting and importing of goods. At this stage he forcefully demanded to be called sir.

### Storeroom in the Basement:
One male presence was detected in here and he had been a solicitor's clerk working in this room, who had died of natural causes in 1860. The team were unable to appropriate a name for this particular presence.

### Second Floor Large Front Office:
The first team established that there was a female presence named Caroline located in this room. She had died of smallpox when she was twenty-four years old after working in the building as a domestic maid.

The second team in contrast found a male presence who had died as recently as 1985, this being of cancer at the age of forty-four. This man had worked here and as the team were processing this information they thought they heard a sound like the tapping of fingers on a keyboard.

They also revealed three other presences that were all male. Very little information was identifiable, however one presence was apparently that of a man who had died in 1897 of natural causes at the age of seventy-three.

### Top Level:
The first team to investigate this area came up with four presences; three of whom were male and one female, though sadly they were unable to reveal information about two of the males.

The female spirit was that of a young girl called Clara or Kara, aged twelve or thirteen and who had died in 1884 of a heart-related disease. She was wearing a blue dress that she had loved.

One of the male spirits had been victim to a horrific and unlawful beheading in 1695. He had been a sailor with strong connections to the smuggling of contraband and had an active role in possessing such illicit items.

The second team were only able to reveal information about a single presence. Nevertheless this was interesting because the information given appeared to bear an uncanny resemblance to a presence identified on the Second Floor. This was again a female named Carolyn, who had had died from smallpox, aged twenty-four.

## Surfside Yellow House

This building, situated in Godrevy Terrace and near the Ayr district of St Ives, is well over 180 years old and a ghostly figure has been seen here on separate occasions and over a period of many years. The owner told me that on one occasion a 'fearless and macho' royal marine had been staying here and one night he got up to go to the toilet in the early hours. However, as he moved across the corridor he suddenly sighted a figure moving along it. The problem being the fact that nobody could possibly have been in that part of the building and the man was so unnerved that he immediately ran back to his room. In the morning he was still so petrified he couldn't even remember if he'd managed to go to the toilet or not in the end. The owner is convinced that this was evidently the ghost that was regularly reported in the building though nobody is clear as to who or what this is.

## Tate, St Ives

This impressive construction was built in 1993 over the site of a former gas works and occupies a fine position with spectacular views right across St Ives and over the ocean and beaches. It was originally constructed to offer the public an opportunity to see exhibitions from well-known artists of the area and, in many cases, this would actually be where the works were created as many of the artists lived very close to where the building is today. As the Tate website states:

> The three storey building backs directly into the cliff face, with a dramatic 50ft drop from cliff-top to beach. The rooftop restaurant has views extending over the rooftops of the town and its harbour out to sea, along the horizon from Clodgy Point over St Ives Bay to the Godrevy Lighthouse. The Porthmeor Beach elevation and the interior detailing, however, reflect the modernist tradition central to the art of St Ives, with interrelated geometric forms, white walls and simple wood and slate finishes. The architects have said that they hope that a visit to the Gallery will feel like an extension of visiting the town itself.

It is a former worker of the gasworks that some people have claimed haunts the Tate Gallery, though it is difficult to substantiate the authenticity of this. A gent in a blue boiler suit has been reportedly seen and several people have claimed to feel an icy-cold touch on the back of their shoulders, when nobody is anywhere near them. It has been further claimed to me that people have gone into the building with no knowledge of this story and seen a dirty and scruffy looking individual in such a uniform. Some people have apparently said good morning to him and been a little put out when he subsequently ignores them. On further examination they have then

*Tate, St Ives*

Opposite: *Surfside Yellow House*

discovered that no such individual is in the building. The story goes on to say that this is reputed to be a man who worked in the gasworks and tragically was killed in an accident where he got caught up in machinery and died. His fellow workers apparently also regularly saw him and recognised him, indeed in life he was renowned for being dirty and scruffy. Naturally enough this is not a story that is officially endorsed by the gallery itself and may therefore not be true. Nevertheless I for one would be intrigued by the idea of such a building, that in name and in ethos is the very essence of modernity, actually having such an old fashioned thing like a ghost – how quaint an idea!

# Towednack, Church

There is a bizarre. old and universal legend relating to the village church at Towednack, a village just a few miles from St Ives. The church, which at one time was known as the Chapel of St Ewin, was dedicated to St Tewinnoc, and is well worth a visit with its unusual squat tower and isolated location. Inside there is a thirteenth-century chancel arch, an early granite altar slab and an ancient carved cross. Outside there are two crosses, one on either side of the medieval porch and in there is a peculiar stone bench made from the shaft of an ancient cross. There can also be found Norman masonry in one of the walls of the nave. The church walls are of great blocks of granite, and the low massive tower, built in the fourteenth century, makes it look rather like a fortress.

Fable dictates that the Devil himself is responsible for the peculiarity of the squat church. When the church was being built, the stonemasons laid the granite blocks during the day and, when they returned the next morning, they had been moved. The story claimed that the Devil had paid a visit to the church during the hours of darkness and knocked it all down each and every night, carrying off the pinnacles and battlements. The builders kept rebuilding day after day but on each occasion the same thing happened once more. Eventually the builders admitted defeat and in despair left the tower shorter and squatter than it was planned to be.

Also associated with the church is the proverb 'there are no cuckolds in Towednack, because there are no horns on the church tower'.

# Trencrom Hill

Also known as Trecobben Hill Fort, this is one of my favourite locales and the steep and tiring climb up is well worth it for a glimpse of the views across the countryside. Originally said to be the site of an old Iron Age hill fort, the summit is associated with the so-called Spriggans – ancient spirits of the mine who are said to be mischievous imps who cause trouble and make a general nuisance of themselves. Some say the spirits of the ancient hill tribes may also haunt the prominence and others say Iron Age soldiers.

There have indeed been many peculiar incidents described at this place over the years. In the 1960s there were four people driving past in a car when all of a sudden their car's engine died. As they tried to restart the vehicle they noticed a figure coming down the hill, stopping a few yards away and just stared at them. As they looked, wondering why, the figure simply vanished. At this point the car restarted immediately and not surprisingly they quickly drove away. At other times people have described a similar figure seen wearing dark and rough clothing.

There have also been sightings of a lady in a long dress seen walking across the nearby road. On one occasion she glided straight through a passing car to the understandable horror of the

*Towednack Church*

*Trencrom Hill*

three travellers inside. Some have linked her to the legend of 'the spirit of the vow' a phantom who the sighting of which will purportedly predict trouble ahead.

On the hill itself a lot of people have described the feeling of being watched and a lot of dogs have been known to react aggressively or as if scared. Also blue lights are a familiar sighting on the hill late at night.

According to the famous Victorian folklorist Robert Hunt, the following story took place sometime over 100 years ago at Trencrom:

One night a local man, believing there to be buried treasure, headed to this enchanted hill on a moonlit night and began to dig into the earth with a spade and pick. He continued to dig for some time believing he would soon find the riches. The sky was swiftly covered with the darkest clouds, shutting out the luminous light of the moon leaving the man in total and unearthly shadows. The wind rose and roared amidst the rocks; but this was soon drowned amidst the terrifying crashes of thunder and flashes of lightning. At this point, the spriggans appeared in swarms from out of the rocks. They were in innumerable numbers; and they rapidly increased in size, until eventually they assumed an almost gigantic form, looking all the while, 'as ugly as if they would eat him'. How this poor man escaped is unknown, but he is said to have been so frightened that he took to his bed, and was not able to work for a long time.

Trencrom was also one of several places in Cornwall reputed to have been a residence for a giant and this particular one apparently enjoyed playing games with the giant of St Michael's Mount. The abundance of boulders strewn across the landscape are reported to be evidence of this. Apparently the two giants would play a game similar to hurling or bob-buttons. The Mount was the 'bob', on which flat masses of granite were placed to serve as buttons, and Trecrobben Hill was the 'mit' or the spot from which the throw was made. This order was sometimes reversed. Hunt again explains that the giants built a castle and mighty blocks were piled upon each other. There the giant chieftains dwelt and dragged their captives up the hill and on the great flat rocks within the castle they sacrificed them. Their gold and jewels were hidden deep in the granite caves and secured by potent spells and they are securely preserved, even to the present day, and carefully guarded from man by the Spriggans or Trolls.

The hill has therefore always held a place in local superstition and, in 1883, *The Cornishman* newspaper wrote, 'Superstitions die hard'. A horse died the other day on a farm in the neighbourhood of St Ives. Its carcase was dragged on a Sunday away up to the granite rock basins and weather-worn bosses of Trecroben hill, and there burnt, in order to drive away the evil spell, or ill-wishing, which afflicted the farm where the animal belonged'.

In 2005 an investigation team came here and found the following information:

* They found the area had strong energy lines, which stretched from St Michael's Mount to the Knill Monument. Also strong residual energy was also found around the rocky outcrops.
* They identified that the area may have been used for Pagan rituals and could also have had some connection to the Druids.
* Several people picked up on soldiers fighting in this area, but many of the presences seemed to be in visitation. The soldiers seemed to be moving all over the area fighting in a long-past battle.

# Unidentified Hotel

Unfortunately I cannot reveal the name of this hotel but I have had the pleasure of carrying out an all-night investigation here a few years ago and I will include a summary of this and also that of a later investigation.

I also had an e-mail from a lady a few years ago, asking if I knew anything about the haunting of this hotel. Her husband had stayed in Room Three in November 2002 and had woken up one morning to witness a woman, with her back to him, gazing from the window, as if out to sea. The lady was also seemingly pointing towards the water. He rose from the bed and started heading towards this lady and as he reached where she was standing, she simply vanished.

There is also believed to be a room haunted by a young child. People staying there with children have often witnessed toys flying around and it was believed to have once been the nursery.

In February 2004 a team of investigators from the PRO were invited into investigate the hotel and came up with some interesting results:

On the first-floor stairs by the fire exit, near Room 128, a psychic picked up on a presence named Mrs Clark who had been a housekeeper at this location and who had died in 1878. He sensed that she was somewhat indignant and moves around the hotel; indeed she was picked up at various times during the investigation and in separate places.

They also picked up on a male presence on the higher stairs. This appeared to be a man who visited here and was 'well to do'. The psychic came up with the name Thomas Craze.

During the investigation the team paused outside Room Three and a male presence was picked up here. According to the psychic the name given was Isaac Pierce (or Pearce) and he had been aged thirty-six and died in the 1660s.

The team then proceeded to a cottage in the grounds, where the psychic also picked up on a presence in a bedroom. This turned out to be Mrs Clark again and it was discovered that she had died in her sixties and had lived here in the latter part of her life, dying from old age. She had been born in Lelant and went on to work at the big house; on retirement she had been allowed to live in this cottage. When she had still been alive she had been married but had no children. Her husband had died before her and had worked the grounds as a farmer (note: later research revealed that there were indeed previously farms here on the same land). Mrs Clark indicated that she had only seen her husband once a week when they were alive and the farm had been part of the estate and her husband had lived above the stables.

On returning to the hotel the psychic confirmed that he could pick up only four presences in the whole building. These were Mrs Clark, Isaac Pearce, Thomas Craze and a Mr Stephens (of whom no information was forthcoming). After speaking to the night porter the team learnt that he was only aware of one ghost story being attached to the building. Allegedly a couple had been staying here and the husband went out for the day. His wife then entertained her lover, expecting her husband not to return however he did come back early and found them in a compromising position. His rage led him to kill both of them and his wife is supposed to haunt the building to this day. The alternative story says he threw his wife off the roof of the building, though the porter did not know when this might have happened. This story does seem to bear a close association to the tale I was told and included above.

Almost exactly two years later a second team went in and investigated a wider area. Please note: the team consisted of completely different investigators. What follows is information picked up from the three independent teams:

*Lodge Three:*
The dowser from the first team reported no spirit presence in this lodge, however orbs were caught on camera and odd EMF readings were gauged over the bed, this may have been due to underground cables.

The second team also said that no presences were to be found in this area at the time of investigation. They also measured high EMF readings, which might suggest a rational explanation. They did also notice that the bedroom was considerably colder than the rest of the lodge and failed to explain this obviously.

*Lodge Four:*
The first team picked up on a spirit presence called Mrs Clark and further felt that this presence was happy, had been married and had worked here.

The second team were dowsing in the living room when they picked up on two presences. Furthermore a male presence, aged about twelve was also found in the hallway with a date of passing around 1771.

The third team picked up on significantly more information from this area but also interestingly identified three presences in the hallway and lounge, this being a female and two male.

The male presence in the lounge was called Charles, aged seventeen and passed through illness.

The female presence in the lounge had died during childbirth in 1773, aged fifteen years old. She was connected to the land but not the present building.

The male presence in the hallway conjured up the most intriguing information, as this closely matched the second team's findings. They also stated that this was a twelve-year-old boy who had died in the late eighteenth century. They also added that he had died due to an accident.

### Garden Cottage One:
One team investigated this are and found a male presence in the upstairs lounge. He had died of heart condition in 1890 at the age of forty and his name was Joseph Andrews. He had lived in the property and was apparently unhappy at the team being there and was telling them to leave.

Interestingly, another investigator then independently dowsed and picked up on a male presence who died in 1888 and he thought his name began with a J, so very similar.

### Garden Cottage Two:
The first team once again used dowsing and revealed three presences, a male and two females.

The first female was called Elizabeth but preferred to be called Beth and had been was married she had also lived in the area before dying from heart problems at the age of fifty-nine.

The second female was called Heather and died aged thirty-three, from natural causes. She had had lived here on the land in 1874, before the hotel was built.

The male presence was not very forthcoming, but the team were given the name Davis. He had worked on the land and had died at the age of thirty-three or thirty-four, as a result of being trampled to death by a horse. This male also had a connection to Beth, it was felt that she might have been his mother. The male presence apparently kept moving about the room and several members felt cold draughts at the same time. One of the investigators claimed that he had seen a dark shadow in the kitchen area.

The second team to investigate this area picked up incredibly similar information to the first one. They also picked up on Beth, who had died of a heart attack but adding in the surname Sutherland and that she had worked and lived on the land. Furthermore they picked up identical information about Heather and the male called Davis.

### Room Three:
The first team to come into this room immediately commented that they would not like to sleep in this room, as they felt it was oppressive. Dowsing then revealed information about a male and a female presence. They further suggested that the female presence had been drowned at sea by her husband, possibly as the result of what we would today call a 'love triangle'.

The second team also picked up on one male and one female presence in this room.

### Room Eighty:
An investigator placed a dictaphone in this room with results that were described as interesting, with several unaccountable sounds.

This room was described, by the first team, as having an unpleasant feeling and dowsing revealed three presences; a female, a male and a small boy, who were all related; father, mother and son. The father had sadly killed both his wife and son by suffocating them. The team were unfortunately unable to substantiate a reason why the man would commit such a desperate and heinous act.

A date of 1861 was revealed, thus suggesting that these presences are indeed associated with the land, rather than the hotel itself, due to the dates involved.

The team said that the mother died at the age of thirty-two and may in the past have shown herself to both members of staff and hotel guests alike.

The second team picked up on uncannily similar information; again picking up on three presences in the room that simply have to be the same family as the results were strikingly comparable. The second team also retrieved information referring to the murder by suffocation of a wife and son by a man. The ages for the wife and son were very closely matched and intriguingly this team managed to get the ladies name, which was Francis. They also felt that she was nervous and pacing the room because her husband was in the room with her. They further discovered the reasons for her death, which were that she was planning on leaving him. Another significant piece of information this team found was that the man was called Edward and died of natural causes aged sixty-one.

The third team managed to identify a male and female presence within this area. The details were not as closely linked as the other teams, however there was still a significant symmetry with elements of the described findings.

Incredibly all three teams also independently picked up on a negative energy in the bathroom and a number of investigators in both teams felt uncomfortable, believing it to be related to the trauma. There was also equipment failure and other problems within this particular area and the third team carried out a thorough investigation. Various investigators described a number of different experiences within this room, including: hairs on the backs of their neck standing on end, tingling sensations from head to toe, breathing difficulties, noises being heard, feelings of being watched, red orb-like flashing lights seen with the naked eye traversing the room and moving shadowy shapes.

## Room Eighty-Four:
Dowsing in this room revealed a female presence who had been married with children and had worked at the hotel as a cleaner. She had died at the age of eighty from natural causes. As the team were obtaining this information one investigator reported backache and also that his hand was burning. These feelings went as soon as he had left the room.

## Room Eighty-Eight:
Two female presences were identified in this particular room by the team, which investigated it. The first female was named as Amy, who had been married, with no children and had died with heart problems, aged thirty-five.

The second female was named as Elizabeth and she had worked here, living locally. It was then stated that Elizabeth had died because she had been trampled by a horse and may well reveal herself to people, including both staff and guests of the hotel.

## Room Eighty-Nine:
Again the team used their dowsing rods to collect information and found a male presence and a female child who were unconnected. The male presence who may have been called Michael was said to be in an army uniform and was American. He had been forty-four years old when he had died in 1915, during the First World War. It is possible that he may have been a guest here and that he had died of natural causes. The young girl was called Emily Pearce and she lived in the building and died of chest-related problems, probably pneumonia. She was described as being six years old and that she died in 1906.

## Room Ninety:
In this room, the team picked up on two presences: one male and one female. The female presence had been a farmer and had passed in 1763, aged thirty-two. The male presence had died in a car accident in 1961, also aged thirty-two.

*Room 101:*
Dowsing here revealed two female presences. The team had the impression that one of the females was called Gladys and would have been quite elderly. She worked here in the hotel, was married with children and had died from lung problems. The second female, named Catherine, had died from natural causes, aged thirty-six or thirty seven.

*The Bar:*
During a short break in the bar, two of the investigating team both heard footsteps, like a child running. They both felt it had sounded like a child. One of the psychic team described that she felt this was a little girl with blonde hair, cut in a bob, and that she was wearing a brown dress. When another member of the team joined them, he was asked to carry out some dowsing to reveal information and actually concurred with the psychic, despite the fact he had no knowledge as to what had occurred.

Overall it was intriguing to see both the contrast and similarities between three teams who had investigated the hotel areas separately and independently and also to see how this compared with the first investigation team's results some two years previously.

# Wesley Place

There is a particular house in this street that has had a long-standing reputation for being a haunted property and all too frequently over the years, people have failed to live here for more than a very short space of time; this being due to their reported paranormal experiences here.

One resident lady awoke one night to the sight of her bedroom door slowly opening. Then she saw a man slowly walking towards her bed. At the time she was absolutely freezing cold. She described the man as being about seventy years old and wearing a peaked cap and old-fashioned mackintosh coat. He was quite stocky in build and approximately 5ft 8in in height. He also had a round and wrinkled face. As it happens, there was a man who had lived here previously who matched this description exactly. He had lived here and indeed had died in the very bedroom, something that was confirmed by the neighbours. The sightings happened more than once and sometimes as a prelude to this; people would hear the front door open and close, followed by the front room door slowly opening as if by itself. What then followed was an impression appearing on the couch as if someone had just sat down. At other times they would hear the back door open, followed by heavy footsteps ascending the stairs, to the bedroom. Of course there was never anyone there when people went to investigate.

I spoke to a lady who worked here as a cleaner and she often felt and saw things and was absolutely convinced that the place was haunted.

On another occasion a young couple moved in and one night heard the familiar noises. They had a two-month-old baby asleep in the upstairs room and suddenly he started to cry. The parents went upstairs to check on him and, by the time they arrived, found their son smiling up and the cradle gently rocking by itself.

Over the years the house has been up for sale more often than not and very few people live there for any great length of time.

*The Wharf*

# The Wharf

In 1862 a local sloop ship called *The Sally* was wrecked off St Ives. It has been said that, ever since, there have been occasions when people have been standing on the Wharf, between midnight and 1.00 a.m., when they have seen an old-fashioned ship heading across the bay as if going towards Hayle. Nevertheless, the vessel disappears before it is able to get much further, and this is said to be at the spot where *The Sally* went down over 145 years ago. It is claimed that on two separate occasions a local fishing boat has headed out towards this ship and actually managed to get close enough to see the words '*The Sally*' emblazoned on the side before the boat vanished.

If people instantly assume by this juncture that this is a story that can be explained by people who are the worse for wear coming out of the nearby Sloop Inn, then the next part is certainly not going to convince any hardened sceptics that this is a verifiable and indisputable ghost story.

One night a man saw the ship, as described above, and subsequently began walking along the wharf. After a few moments he spotted a man standing, leaning on a nearby pole and with the lateness of the hour spoke a pleasantry to him. However, this man failed to respond and on looking up gave our hero the shock of his life. To his utter disgust he described staring face to face with an extremely ugly man with glaring eyes, a parboiled face and seaweed hanging from the corner of his mouth. He tried to make a swift exit but to his horror found that the man was

*The Wharf*

following him closely behind. Bizarrely he could hear squelching as the man walked each step and at this point finally lost his nerve and ran for home, leaving the grinning, sinister seaman behind. Nevertheless, as he arrived home he was met with his darkest fear, the same figure was already there, standing ahead of him with a sinister and ghastly grin etched across his face. Nowhere does it report what happened then.

# Woolworths

Perhaps not the most obvious location for a ghost story but nevertheless Woolworths has what may well be St Ives longest consistently running ghost story.

About 120 years ago, the building was split into different compartments or units and on the ground floor was a successful business. The owner was a draper and he was described as being a workaholic. He worked very, very hard every day and especially late at night fulfilling orders and jobs. Ultimately, though, it is believed he worked too hard and paid the ultimate price. One night he was up working late, as he always was, when he suddenly had a heart attack. Unfortunately his wife didn't find him until the next morning and by then he was dead. This was especially hard for the family because they not only lost a beloved father and husband but also their only

*Woolworths*

source of income and so very soon they were destitute and had to leave the building, which had been their home for many years.

Soon afterwards there were others who moved into the same part of the building and almost immediately reported strange goings on. This included feelings, objects moving, noises, atmospheres and in particular sightings of a ghostly figure. The figure was described as a man and the description bore an uncanny resemblance to the draper. So unnerved were they by the regular appearances that they moved out. Incredibly, a pattern then emerged, whereby people moved into this part of the property, reported strange goings on and sightings and then left completely convinced that the building was haunted. This went on for many, many years until eventually Woolworths bought the whole building, this being several decades ago.

When the company first moved in, a lot of locals turned and said, 'I wonder how long they'll last', based on the fact that everyone previously had moved out very quickly. Nevertheless Woolworths are still there and this may not be because activity has ceased. I have spoken to several people who have worked there over the years who are absolutely convinced that the building is haunted and many peculiar occurrences have taken place. This has included strange sounds, objects and items of stock being moved overnight in a locked and empty building, electrics playing up, the alarm regularly going off without explanation, feelings of extreme coldness and impressions of being watched. There have also been several sightings and again the descriptions are very similar to the ones, which have now been expressed for over 120 years – seemingly that of the draper. Much of the activity occurs around the area of the staff lift on the ground floor and people have claimed that this is where the draper's workbench might have been situated.

I also recently received a letter from some people who had an experience in Woolworths themselves. This is what one of them wrote in her own words:

> I was in Woolworths store buying birthday cards when I was near the lift. I started spinning round like I was on a hoola hoop and couldn't get off. My husband was at the other end of the store so I asked him to come and stand beside me, which he did. Nothing happened to him but I started spinning again in the same way and it didn't stop until I moved away from the lift. I thought you might like to know this. I can only put it down to the fact that maybe the ghost knows I have been a seamstress in my time and like sowing.

# Zennor, St Senara's Church

This Norman, granite church probably stands on the site of a sixth-century Celtic church. Two medieval bench ends remain and have been made into a seat. One end is the famous carving of the Mermaid of Zennor, holding a comb and a mirror in her hands. On the south side of the church tower is a bronze dial bearing the figure of a mermaid, and an inscription dated 1737. There is a coffin rest at the gate to the church. This dates from the time when the dead might have to be carried quite a distance in their coffins to the church. Before the coffin was carried into the church, it was placed on the coffin rest for a time. The pallbearers sat on the stone benches alongside to rest.

The title Zennor is thought to have come from St Senara, a name linked with the Breton Princess Asenora who, according to legend, was falsely accused by her stepmother of infidelity and thus sentenced to burning. However, when it was discovered she was pregnant, her jailers threw her into the sea in a barrel, rather than be responsible for murdering an unborn child. She is said to have floated to Ireland, being fed by an angel along the way. However, she eventually decided to return to Brittany with her son Budoc and stopped off to found Zennor.

. Nonetheless, the church is best known for the very famous legend of the Mermaid of Zennor, depicted in the aforementioned bench end (as pictured) and described as a beautiful woman, with long golden hair and sea-green eyes, wearing a shimmering long silver dress. The original story claims she made a visit to the church on Sunday mornings during services many centuries ago. She would quietly enter the church, just as the service began and sat herself at the back, near the door, as far away from the congregation as was possible. But one day she caught the gaze of a young male member of the choir called Matthew Trewella and on each visit would look longingly into his eyes. At the end of the service she would leave quickly and sometimes be seen speedily heading in the direction of the cliffs, near Vear Cove. She never spoke to anyone but very soon Matthew became bewitched by her beauty and became obsessed with the thought of making her acquaintance. In return, many believed the beautiful young woman was equally spellbound by Matthew and was retuning every Sunday to look at him and to hear his singing. After several months, on one autumn Sunday, Matthew made the decision that he would leave the service early in order to meet his beloved and thus waited outside the church. As the lady

*Zennor, St Senara's Church*

*Zennor, St Senara's Church*

*Zennor, St Senara's Church*

left, he followed her towards the cliff and as they reached the edge she turned and gazed straight at him. He spoke to her and they continued onwards, until she was seen entering the sea with Matthew following. Quickly the ocean swallowed them and his family never saw Matthew again. It was only then that people realised that he had fallen under the spell of a mermaid.

Apparently some years later a ship was passing by the same coastline when it dropped anchor in order to collect supplies from the neighbouring farms. Suddenly they heard a sweet woman's voice coming form what appeared to be the sea. The captain listened and heard the words 'Captain will you haul up your anchor for 'tis blocking the door of my cave. I can't get inside to Matthew and our children'. The startled captain did as he was instructed and the voice disappeared.

This has become an incredibly famous story, attracting thousands of people to Zennor every year, many of whom are hoping for their own brief glimpse of a mermaid.

## Zennor, Foage Lane

On the edge of Zennor is a winding lane, which leads onto Foage Farm. A lot of people who have been walking in this lane have claimed to experience a feeling of ill ease and there are few who will venture here after dark. Two people once saw a ghostly figure riding up the lane on a bicycle, described as a gentleman in Victorian clothing, covered in blood. However this man and the bicycle simply vanished. This could possibly be explained by something that happened at a nearby mine. In the mid-nineteenth century there was a tragedy at nearby Rosevale Tin Mine. A gas cylinder exploded and injured several men, killing one poor soul. The story of the cyclist suggests that this man may have been someone who rode off to get help after the accident.

Also in a nearby cottage there are those who claim a ghostly presence. Most visitors and residents have described this as a friendly female spirit. People often have a feeling of being watched and other sensations. A few years ago a horse coming past the building went into an uncharacteristic panic and ran from the location.

## Zennor, Miller's Cottage

People have felt very uncomfortable in this 200-year-old premises, describing it as evil and full of sadness.

## Zennor, Tinners Arms

This pub is the only such establishment in the beautiful village of Zennor and is a popular watering hole, possibly built in 1271 to house the stonemasons who built the nearby church. During the First World War, D.H. Lawrence and his German wife Frieda stayed at the Tinners Arms and solicited a great deal of suspicion locally before, it is rumoured, being asked to leave by the local police.

It has been haunted for as long anyone can remember with many of the previous landlords having heard footsteps above the bar when the area is empty. This happens particularly at night and usually just after closing time.

On one occasion a large dog became absolutely ferocious during a visit to the pub. He began staring at the ceiling and growling and barking. His teeth were bared and the hackles stood

*Zennor, Tinners Arms*

Opposite: *Zennor, Tinners Arms*

*Zennor Vicarage*

up on the back of his neck. The dog then fled out of the pub and ran away. Glasses and other objects have also been found moved around in the bar. It is claimed that the pub is haunted by a poltergeist who especially becomes alive just before a thunderstorm.

## Zennor Vicarage

A previous rector, who is mainly seen in the bathroom and then witnessed leaving through the bathroom door, allegedly haunts this building. He is said by many to be a very strong presence and despite being a man of the cloth, has been described as an unpleasant character. Apparently years ago someone attempted an exorcism, which was unsuccessful.

For more information about taking part in a ghost walk around the town of St Ives, with the author, go to:

www.ghosthunting.org.uk

and click on ghost walks.

# Other local titles published by The History Press

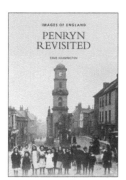

## Penryn Revisited

ERNIE WARMINGTON

Founded in 1216, Penryn stands in a sheltered position at the head of the Penryn River and by the sixteenth century was one of the principal ports in Cornwall. The town prospered with its imports and exports of a wide variety of cargo. Author Ernie Warmington takes the reader on a nostalgic trip into the past. With images depicting all aspects of the town's community, buildings and industrial heritage, this book will delight residents and visitors past and present.

978 07524 4607 3

## Haunted Cornwall

PAUL NEWMAN

For anyone who would like to know why Cornwall is called the most haunted place in Britain, this collection of stories of apparitions, manifestations and related supernatural incidents from around the Duchy provides the answer. From heart-stopping accounts of poltergeists to first-hand encounters with ghouls and spirits who haunt prehistoric graves, Haunted Cornwall contains a chilling range of ghostly phenomena.

978 07524 3668 5

## Haunted Devon

IAN ADDICOAT

This enthralling collection of tales about ghostly Devon contains a chilling range of ghostly tales. From the ghost of Isabella, the illegitimate child of Baron de Pomeroy murdered when she was but nine, to séances at the Smuggler's Haunt, personal messages from Peggy Penny and a ghost tour around Boringdon Hall, this phenomenal gathering of ghostly goings-on is bound to captivate anyone interested in the supernatural history of the county.

978 07524 3977 8

## Pirates of the West Country

E.T. FOX

Discover the handful of true West Country pirates of the past and also those that voyaged from the West to the Caribbean and Indian Ocean in this compelling history. Herein lies a true account of piracy, often called the 'oldest trade afloat'. Indeed, it is older than the golden age represented in the literature of Stevenson and Barrie, and more widespread than portrayed by Hollywood. These true tales of pirates operating from places such as Lulworth Cove, Plymouth Hoe and Corfe Castle inspired the pirate fiction we know today.

978 07524 4377 5

If you are interested in purchasing other books published by The History Press, or in case you have difficulty finding any of our books in your local bookshop, you can also place orders directly through our website
www.thehistorypress.co.uk